Norman T. Carrington MA

Brodie's Notes on William Shakespeare's

King Lear

Pan Educational London and Sydney

First published by James Brodie Ltd
This edition published 1976 by Pan Books Ltd,
Cavaye Place, London SW10 9PG
2   3   4   5   6   7   8   9
© James Brodie Ltd. 1962
ISBN 0 330 50011 2
Printed and bound in Great Britain by
Richard Clay (The Chaucer Press) Ltd, Bungay, Suffolk

CONTENTS

KING LEAR

THE AUTHOR

SURPRISINGLY little is known of the life of our greatest dramatist, and the little we know is derived mainly from brief references to his name in legal and other formal documents. He was born in Stratford-on-Avon, and, although the exact date of his birth is unknown, there is a record that he was christened William on 26th April, 1564, the third child of John Shakespeare, a man variously described as glover, wool-dealer, farmer, and butcher. Until about the year 1578, when his business seems to have begun to decline, John Shakespeare was a notable figure in Stratford, and it is probable that William was educated at Stratford Grammar School, where he may have learned the "small Latin and less Greek" for which Jonson gave him credit. However this may be, the next thing we know that can be accepted as reliable is that on 27th November, 1582, he took out a licence for marriage with a certain Anne Whateley. It was annulled next day, however, upon information laid by the sponsors of another Anne (Anne Hathaway) who claimed a better right for her to be married to William, since she was with child by him. At the age of eighteen, therefore, he married Anne Hathaway, a woman eight years older than himself, and by 1585 three children had been born of the marriage. In this year he is thought to have left Stratford for London. Tradition has it that his departure was owing to trouble over deer-stealing in the grounds of Sir Thomas Lucy, but in the light of modern research it would appear that he left with a band of strolling players, the Queen's Players, who visited Stratford in 1585. His unwilling marriage to Anne Hathaway may have had something to do with his decision to leave his native town.

Whether his wife and children ever lived with him in London is not known for certain, but it is very unlikely, nor is it known what he himself did there before 1592. From a pamphlet published in that year by Robert Greene, a lesser dramatist, however, we have news of him as actor and playwright. Plague caused the theatres to be closed

5

in 1593, and on their re-opening in the following year we know that Shakespeare was a member of the Lord Chamberlain's Company (known, after the accession of James I, as the King's Men), and it is probable that he stayed with this company for the remainder of his career, writing plays for it and acting with it in various theatres. His connection with the company must have brought him considerable financial reward, for we know that in 1596 his father, presumably aided by his successful son, applied to the College of Heralds for the right to assume a family coat of arms, and in the following year the playwright purchased (for £60!) New Place, one of the largest houses in Stratford. Although the house is no longer there, the foundations can be seen and the garden is open to the public. As his fortunes prospered, Shakespeare bought shares in two theatres, the Globe, built in 1599, and the Blackfriars, built in 1609, so that, in addition to his pay as actor and writer, he would receive his share of the profits on these investments.

Thus in 1611, when still under fifty years of age, Shakespeare retired to his native town, a fairly wealthy man, though he seems to have kept up a connection with London, as he was concerned in a legal dispute over the purchase of a house in Blackfriars in 1615. He died in Stratford-on-Avon, survived by his wife and two daughters, on 23rd April, 1616, and was buried in the Parish Church, where thousands of people from all over the world visit his grave every year.

As an actor Shakespeare does not seem to have been eminent, but even in his own day his fame as a dramatist was very great. Thus Meres in 1598 described him as "the most excellent in both kinds" (*i.e.* in comedy and in tragedy) and even Ben Jonson, whose dramatic work was in a very different vein from that of Shakespeare, remarks in his *Discoveries*, "I lov'd the man and do honour his memory (on this side idolatry) as much as any".

Shakespeare probably began his work as a dramatist by collaborating with others and patching up old plays which his company wished to revive. His first completely original play is believed to be *Love's Labour's Lost* (1591?), though the date of each play is itself a problem, since the dates are not given in the First Folio (the first collected edition of his plays, 1623). His non-dramatic works consist of two narrative poems, *Venus and Adonis* (1593) and *The Rape of Lucrece* (1594), and the one hundred and fifty-four sonnets published in 1609—without Shakespeare's permission it is thought. The first one hundred and twenty-six of the sonnets are addressed to a young man, the poet's friend and patron; the remainder to a "dark lady", and the identity of neither of these two is established, though it is tempting to believe that the "dark lady" was Anne Whateley; nor is it decided how far, if at all, the series may be considered autobiographical. Most of Shakespeare's plays were written for performance in the public playhouses, and they were conveniently classified in the First Folio in three groups—comedies, histories, and tragedies. But when considered chronologically they seem to fall naturally into four periods, thus admirably described by Professor Dowden.

First, from about 1590 to 1595-96, years of dramatic apprenticeship and experiment; secondly, from about 1595-96 to about 1600-01, the period of the English historical plays and the mirthful and joyous comedies; thirdly, from 1601 to about 1608, the period of grave and bitter comedies and of the great tragedies; last, from about 1608 to 1611 or 1613, the period of the romantic plays, which are at once grave and glad, serene and beautiful.*

Professor Dowden names these periods respectively "In the workshop", "In the world", "Out of the depths", "On the heights". *King Lear* belongs to the period of the great tragedies, and all the evidence points to late 1605 or early 1606 as the date of its composition.

* *Shakspere Primer*, p. 47, pub. Messrs. Macmillan and Co. Ltd., whose permission for its reproduction is hereby thankfully acknowledged.

THE PLAY

PLOT

King Lear, a powerful king in declining years, decides that it is time to hand over his kingdom to his three daughters. Through a petty grievance he cuts off his youngest daughter, Cordelia, who loved him dearly, without a share, deciding to live alternately with the other two.

It is not long before these two elder daughters, Goneril and Regan, use their authority to turn their father out, and then plot for supreme power the one against the other. Another complication is that they are both enamoured of the same man, Edmund, bastard son of the Duke of Gloucester, and Goneril is prepared to have her husband murdered so that she may marry him.

In the end Cordelia, now Queen of France, brings an army to fight for her father against his oppressors. It is defeated, but the figure-heads of the victorious army meet death in their hour of victory, for Goneril poisons Regan and then commits suicide. Those remaining determine that right shall be done, but not before Cordelia is hung in prison and Lear dies over her dead body.

Parallel with this the Duke of Gloucester's illegitimate younger son, Edmund, tricks his father into believing that his elder son and heir, Edgar, is false to him. As a punishment for aiding Lear, Gloucester has his eyes cut out, with the connivance of Edmund, who seeks his lands and title, and in his affliction he is afterwards succoured by Edgar (in disguise), who ultimately kills his step-brother in a duel.

These events are the mere skeleton of the play, and in them rests nothing of the greatness of *King Lear*.

SOURCE OF PLOT AND TREATMENT

The story of King Lear is an old legend that is told in several places, but Shakespeare undoubtedly read it in Holinshed's *Chronicles of England, Scotland and Ireland*, of which he made much use in his history plays, and saw it in a play called *King Leir and his Three Daughters* (1588).

King Lear is the only Shakespearean Tragedy with a sub-plot. The Gloucester story he found in Sidney's

Arcadia, Book II, where it is told of "the Paphlagonian unkinde king, and his kind sonne".

These two stories have no connection, of course, outside our play. As usual, Shakespeare treats his source with great freedom. First of all he intertwined a sub-plot with the Lear plot in order to make the severance of natural family relationships more universal, and therefore more realistic, for it is easier to believe in the one because the other has taken place.

The most striking thing about our *King Lear,* however, is that the most tragic elements are Shakespeare's own. In the old play and in Holinshed the army of Cordelia is victorious and Lear is restored to his kingdom. At the turn of the seventeenth century a Nahum Tate dressed up *King Lear* with a happy ending. This is what Charles Lamb said about it.

A happy ending!—as if the living martyrdom that Lear had gone through,—the flaying of his feelings alive, did not make a fair dismissal from the stage of life the only decorous thing for him. If he is to live and be happy after, if he could sustain this world's burden after, why all this pudder and preparation,—why torment us with all this unnecessary sympathy? As if the childish pleasure of getting his gilt robes and sceptre again could tempt him to act over again his misused station,—as if at his years, and with his experience, anything was left but to die!

To take a more practical view, Shakespeare would have to consider in addition the effect on his audience of a French victory on British soil. A further tragic element is that only in Shakespeare does Lear go mad.

Of course, there is nothing in either "source" of Shakespeare's characterisation. A mere succession of events becomes in his hands a story with cause and effect, *due to human character.* Lear and Gloucester themselves are responsible for the misfortunes that come upon them. A spent old man in the old play is here a powerful figure who makes a fatal mistake owing to a weakness in his character. All the important characters are more complex, more as we know men and women to be in real life. The Cordelia of the old play is not so blunt as Shakespeare's Cordelia, but the two elder sisters incline their father's heart against her. If Shakespeare followed this it would be too much like his sub-plot, where Edmund manages to displace Edgar from his father's affection. In Holinshed and the old play Lear gives Goneril and Regan in marriage because he is well-pleased with their answers, in Shakespeare they are already married. It brings variety that they are married and Cordelia is not. In Shakespeare only is there a rival to the King of France for Cordelia's love, and this sets off her attractiveness and also shows the dramatic contrast that without a penny she is to be happier in her love than she would have been with all Lear's gifts (when she would have become the wife of a man who wanted her for her money).

The banishment of Lear's counsellor (Kent) in Shakespeare shows his character—he will remain in the hope of helping Lear, even if it imperils himself. It shows Lear's character too, in times gone by, for only a good king could have inspired such devotion in such a man. And the faithful Fool, who follows Lear like a dog at heel, is entirely Shakespeare's conception, a subtle blend of humour and pathos, emphasising the helplessness of man.

Shakespeare introduces the additional complication of the rivalry of Goneril and Regan for the love of Edmund, which shows that their alliance is entirely self-centred and in the structure of the play links the main and the sub-plot more closely together.

Shakespeare's contribution is everything that makes the play great literature, that takes the story of this individual character and makes it universal—related to the character of all of us, so that the play becomes a grim piece of dramatic symbolism representing types of humanity, who are at the same time particularised as individual men and women (not just qualities, as in the morality plays). The struggle in the play is a symbol of the struggle between good and evil in the world, always remembering that goodness and evil are non-existent apart from good and evil men and women. Crude and improbable legends become real and lifelike and move us when we feel our kinship with the actors. Holinshed and the play of *King Leir and his Three Daughters* would be forgotten if Shakespeare had not used them, and are remembered only so far as they show his method. Shakespeare's play is of value to the student of human nature. A story with a "realistic" plot has no life if the characters are wooden, but a crude plot becomes alive when living people inform it. It is in his *treatment* of the plot that Shakespeare shows his imagination. Artistic creation bears the same relation to plot as architecture to bricks and mortar.

And great literature means great writing. Shakespeare's sources have a quaint appeal to modern ears, but their language does not touch our feelings and a re-reading is pointless (that is, apart from the study of Shakespeare). Once we know their story they have done for us all they can. We can read *King Lear* again and again, and each time it says something new, and its power and its terror and its glory move us afresh.

PARALLELISM AND INTERACTION OF PLOT AND SUB-PLOT

MAIN PLOT

I. i. With incredible stupidity Lear takes a sudden hatred to a beloved daughter and attaches himself to two worthless ones, owing to a weakness in his character. A momentary impulse outweighs years of affection. From this error, and its attendant circumstances, spring the calamities that befall him.

SUB-PLOT

I. ii. With incredible stupidity Gloucester takes a sudden hatred to a beloved son and attaches himself to a worthless one, owing to a weakness in his character, and from this error spring the calamities that befall him. The reasons for Edmund's jealousy are plain from Gloucester's nonchalant introduction of him in a short conversation at the start of I. i.

Edmund tells Gloucester that he has often heard Edgar "maintain it to be fit, that, sons at perfect age, and father declining, the father should be as ward to the son, and the son manage his revenue", which is just what Lear has arranged in his kingdom (except that he was going to be as ward to his daughters), and the King's action makes his son's villainy more believable.—"This villain of mine comes under the prediction; there's son against father: the king falls from bias of nature; there's father against child."

These two opening scenes are dramatic in themselves and big with consequences for the future.

Kent banished.

II. i. Edgar banished.

II. i. Lear's servant (the banished Kent) insulted at Glouces-

III. iii. Gloucester's sympathy for Lear, communicated to Edmund,

ter's castle, and Gloucester pleads for him.

iv. Lear leaves Gloucester's castle and the doors are locked against him.

III. iv. Lear's real madness is made worse by coming into contact with Edgar, who only feigns madness. Hazlitt draws attention to the distinction between the two, while the resemblance in the cause of their distress keeps up a unity of interest.

Lear's "redemption", *e.g.* III. iv. 23-36.

iv. Lear will consent to go into the farmhouse only if Edgar goes too.

In disguise the banished Kent helps Lear.

III. vii. Cornwall's death comes by reason of his cruelty to Gloucester.

IV. ii. Goneril makes a confession of love for Edmund, but soon afterwards hears that Regan is a widow and hence is free to marry him.

v. The rivalry of Goneril and Regan for Edmund's love becomes apparent and ultimately results in the death of both of them.

vi. The victims of each plot meet. Gloucester can hear but not see Lear, and it is some time before Lear recognises Gloucester.

vii. Lear is cared for by Cordelia.

V. i. Goneril's wish to rid herself of Albany in favour of Edmund is revealed by Edgar (after he has slain Goneril's servant, Oswald).

leads to his blindness. Sympathy for his father's blindness lends vigour to Edgar's sword at the end.

III. vii. Gloucester gets his eyes put out and is turned out of his own castle (in favour of Edmund) for helping Lear, his service to whom was betrayed by Edmund.

Gloucester says, "Thou say'st the king grows mad! I'll tell thee, friend, I am almost mad myself".

Gloucester's "redemption", *e.g.* IV. i. 15-17, 69-73. Also Edgar's sympathy with Lear, III. vi. 102-110.

IV. i. Hence Edgar is near to his father when he needs help.

In disguise the banished Edgar helps Gloucester.

vi. Gloucester is cared for by Edgar.

iii. Cordelia is slain by Edmund's orders. As a result Lear dies of shock.

V. iii. Gloucester dies of shock at the revelation of Edgar's truth (and Edmund's treachery). Gloucester dies off the stage, as otherwise it would have made Lear's death appear an anticlimax to his.

At the end, Albany, the only survivor (except France, in whom no one is interested) of the Lear group, confers with Edgar, the only survivor of the Gloucester group, about the welfare of the state in the years immediately ahead.

In any play there is a clash of personalities or of wills. This it is that makes the play. Within the structure of these two parallel plots, notice the clashes.

1. Between armies of different nations.

2. Between rival groups for mastery in the same country.

3. In families.

4. Between individual characters. Character-contrast is a fundamental principle in Shakespearean drama.

5. In men's hearts and minds, *e.g.* Lear, when he thinks of the wrong he has done Cordelia.

6. Between puny man and the strength and vastness of the physical forces of the universe (III. ii).

ATMOSPHERE AND THEME

The theme of the play is the relationship of parents and children, with particular emphasis on the ungrateful child.

> Ingratitude, thou marble-hearted fiend,
> More hideous when thou show'st thee in a child
> Than the sea-monster!

> How sharper than a serpent's tooth it is
> To have a thankless child!

Ingratitude is the quality of mankind uppermost in Lear's mind; again in the storm the thought returns to him, and he calls upon the "all-shaking thunder" to "spill at once" all "germens" "that make ingrateful man".

But before the end of the play we learn that the love of a good child can be mightier than death. Without Cordelia's death the greatness of the sacrifice which her love of her father made her willing to risk would have been hidden.

Really there is only one tragic theme—the helplessness of man. *Lear* is a typical Shakespearean tragedy: it is not a tragedy of bad luck, but a tragedy where man's helplessness springs from human character—good or bad, his own or somebody else's. The tragedy of Lear, it is true, springs from the cruelty of Goneril and Regan, but it would never have happened if Lear had not been foolish and conceited and if Cordelia had not felt that she must stand up and be true to herself (see Cordelia's character, pp. 24-25).

King Lear shows the relentlessness of life. There is no "poetic justice". Some are taken and some are left, irrespective of their deserts.

Much has been written on the meaning of pain in the world. Shakespeare did not write on such abstract themes —he presented them in action in a flash. In *King Lear* the king who fails is made better by his suffering, and his enemies who succeed are made worse by their success.

The atmosphere of the play is wild and barbarous, ruthless and primitive. On the stage we see a man's eyes gouged out, and even when we know that it is coming it still sends a shudder through the theatre. We see a man driven mad by his sufferings in a night of storm and terror, a father thrown out of doors by his *daughters*. In *King Lear* people follow their impulses like savages, with no sense of restraint or mastery of self. The normal ties of civilised life are broken—loyalty to one's family and one's country. And the pathos of it all when the chief character in the play feels that even his pet dogs have turned against him.

> The little dogs and all,
> Tray, Blanch, and Sweetheart, see, they bark at me.

It is interesting to note, adding to the savage character of the play, that the gods are mentioned many times, but God only once. Certain Christian customs are, however, alluded to; for example, Edgar is Lear's godson, and Kent's determination to "eat no fish" may be his way of saying that he is no Papist.

The student should also notice how the animal imagery emphasises the savage character of the play. If he makes a list of the animals mentioned he will find that they are nearly all wild or repulsive creatures.

"Men are as the time is," says one who has risen to high place by treachery in this savage world. But not all are so, and *King Lear* contains one of the most beautiful characters in all Shakespeare, one "who redeems nature from the general curse", who, paradoxically enough, by her own loveliness of character emphasises the cruelty and ugliness of others.

SETTING

The local colour of all Shakespeare's plays is that of Elizabethan England, whether the story is one of Ancient Britain, Denmark or Egypt, and in whatever age. Nowadays we should demand strict accuracy in scenery, costume and topical references, but then, for playwright and audience alike, the life and spirit of a play mattered more than strict accuracy in local colour. "It is the spirit which giveth life." People saw in the drama a reflection of their own life and experience; its appeal was in no wise analytical or educational, but human and curiously personal.

Further, in those days people were untravelled and uneducated, and anachronisms would not strike a false note in an age more familiar with the stories than with their settings.

And it must be remembered that there was no scenery and no period costume. Incongruities which become apparent beside "realistic" scenery would not be noticed then, and references to a character's dress must be to something that he was actually wearing on the stage.

King Lear takes place nominally in Ancient Britain, but, in spite of the half-civilised atmosphere and tone, we are never very far from the England that Shakespeare knew. The local colour is essentially Elizabethan. Letters are thrown in at casement windows, the King has a "fool" who wears a "coxcomb" and who is threatened with the whip, armies march with drum and colours, rules of duelling are strictly observed, Bedlam beggars terrorise country people and criminals are hunted in the way with which everyone in the audience was familiar (II. i. 80-83). Edgar knows the way to Dover "both stile and gate, horse-way and foot-path" (IV. i), and "wakes and fairs and market-towns" are a feature of Britain of the day (III. vi). Kent's contemptuous description of a serving-man has a strongly Elizabethan flavour (II. ii).

What is undoubtedly a reference in *King Lear* to something in people's minds at the time the play was first produced is indicated in the note to "these late . . . moon", p. 55. People then had a superstitious reverence for the stars, which, they believed, had a power over human life and character. The Fool's reference to a monopoly, in which "lords and great men" had an interest, has a similar topical ring, for the granting of monopolies (often in return for a money gift) was a scandal which lasted until 1624.

SYMPATHETIC BACKGROUND

Sympathetic background is rather different from local background. It is an old device, and is universal, from the greatest literature to the cheapest films, whereby the weather is harmonised with the events in the story, at once intensifying the atmosphere and broadening it, as if not only the group of people in the story were affected but the whole universe. The strife and turmoil of the "all-shaking thunder" on the heath echo the strife and turmoil in Lear's kingdom, in his family, and in his mind and heart—unparalleled disturbance in the world of nature (Kent can never remember a night like it, III. ii. 40-43) and unparalleled disturbance in the world of man. Lear himself connects the two as he faces the elements (III. ii. 19-24, III. iv. 6-9, 11-14).

The student would do well to note the amount of *King Lear* that happens at night-time or in a dark place (all Act III, besides scenes in other acts), and the number of references to darkness (*e.g.* "Darkness and devils!" I. iv). The cruel deeds of *King Lear* will not bear the light of day. In this the play is similar to *Macbeth*, which followed it. Incidentally, Duncan too is murdered on the worst night in living memory.

CHARACTERS

King Lear

> You see me here, you gods, a poor old man,
> As full of grief as age; wretched in both!

The very idea of dividing the kingdom "that future strife may be prevented now" shows Lear's lack of shrewdness: in normal circumstances this would be just the way to provide for three states striving against one another for mastery. Before the play opens Lear has already made the division—

"We *have* divided in three our kingdom", and it is common knowledge among the lords at court (*e.g.* Kent, Gloucester and Burgundy). The idea that his daughters shall be awarded their portion according to their expressions of love is just a pretext to indulge his love of flattery. If two portions of the kingdom had already been disposed of, it is obvious that the remaining (and larger) portion could not be distributed according to the recipient's protestation of love. Lear knew that Cordelia loved him best. The unexpected rebuff where he had expected the greatest avowal of love made him suddenly go to the other extreme and cast Cordelia off for ever as his "*sometime* daughter". As Coleridge said, "To be wroth with one we love doth work like madness in the brain".* Cordelia was his best beloved daughter. He says as much and it is obvious from his attitude. He addresses Goneril as "our eldest born", Regan as "our dearest Regan", but Cordelia as "our *joy*". In addition, the sensible Kent, who bade Lear think twice, is banished, and, most despicable of all, France is dissuaded from marrying Cordelia.

> Therefore beseech you
> To avert your liking a more worthier way
> Than on a wretch whom nature is ashamed
> Almost to acknowledge hers.

A shocking exhibition of temper. Lear is an old man past his best, but old age cannot exculpate such offences. As an absolute monarch he has always been accustomed to have his own way, and now he is losing common sense in his judgment of what that way ought to be. His character is the same out of office as in it, with a weakening of his mental balance.

The best and soundest of his time hath been but rash; then must we look to receive from his age, not alone the imperfections of long-ingrafted condition, but therewithal the unruly waywardness that infirm and choleric years bring with them (Goneril).

It would appear from Regan's next remark that such "unconstant starts" "as this of Kent's banishment" had not been a common occurrence in the past. The real reason for Lear's casting off Cordelia "Without our grace, our love, our benison", he unconsciously acknowledges himself—"Better thou hadst not been born *than not to*

Christabel, ll. 412-413.

have pleased me better". Her rebuff has wounded his pride, and he takes it out of her in vindictive resentment, mad with rage even before his mind is turned, and unfortunately he has the power to make the wild impulses of his rage effective. Goneril and Regan satisfy his whim, and alongside this personal satisfaction he takes them at their word and cannot see through the hypocrisy of these two daughters. Such a nature lives on appearances, and even in the act of giving up the responsibility of kingship Lear wishes to retain the "name and all the additions to a king"— the show, the pomp and circumstance, the bowing and scraping that surrounds authority, an authority, be it noticed, that he will no longer possess. When he banishes Kent he talks about "our potency made good", forgetting that he has relinquished his "potency". Coleridge draws attention to "Lear's moral incapacity of resigning the sovereign power in the very act of disposing of it".

The part of Lear needs an experienced actor, for the impression given by the play is that, although he is a shadow of his former self, he *has* been a great king in his day— "every inch a king"—and this must be brought home to the audience. He has been able to inspire devotion in an honourable nobleman like Kent, whose past experience leads him to risk discovery in serving him still. Physically he is a fine man. At eighty years of age he goes hunting, lives through exposure to the storm, gives the attendants who have been sent for him a run before they can lay hands upon him (IV. vi), kills the slave who was hanging Cordelia and is able to carry her dead body. So in Milton's *Paradise Lost* do we get the impression that the fallen Satan still retains much of his former power and glory and majesty and pride in place. Charles Lamb goes so far as to say that "the Lear of Shakespeare cannot be acted. The contemptible machinery by which they mimic the storm which he goes out in, is not more inadequate to represent the horrors of the real elements, than any actor can be to represent Lear." The editor, however, while he has seen some Lears not capable of producing the complex impression that Shakespeare intended, has seen Lear well acted, notably at the Royal Shakespeare Theatre, Stratford-on-Avon, and if the part *cannot* be acted then *King Lear* fails as a play.

When Goneril comes out in her true colours (I. iv)

Lear realises how foolish he has been in sending Cordelia away in a fit of temper. When a Knight casually mentions "my young lady's going into France", Lear cuts him short with "No more of that"—he cannot bear to think of it, until in the following scene (I. v), lost in his thoughts while the Fool prattles on, apropos of nothing he comes out with "I did her wrong", showing how the injury he has done her is pressing on his mind. When the Knight draws his attention to the lack of "ceremonious affection" in his entertainment, Lear says, "Thou but rememberest me of mine own conception". He has not mentioned it because he is conscious that he has only himself to blame for it. "Woe, that too late repents," he exclaims after Goneril shows herself, and then he goes on to mention Cordelia by name.

> O most small fault,
> How ugly didst thou in Cordelia show!
> That, like an engine, wrench'd my frame of nature
> From the fix'd place; drew from my heart all love,
> And added to the gall. O Lear, Lear, Lear!
> Beat at this gate, that let thy folly in,   [*Striking his head.*
> And thy dear judgment out!

The realisation of this makes him more angry in desperation, and Goneril's opposition produces an even greater outburst of uncontrollable anger, although he does feel a sense of shame that she has "power to shake my manhood thus". She has never been in a position to threaten her father before, and at first he fails to understand what she means—"Are you our daughter?" Then, when the significance of her words dawns upon him, out come extravagant curses upon her, just as they did upon Cordelia when she displeased him. Regan knows him well—"So will you wish on me, when the rash mood is on" (II. iv)—better indeed than he knows her.

He still fancies that he has somewhere to go, someone to take care of him, the one remaining string on his lyre that Hope clings to, as in Watts's famous picture. How ironically pathetic it is, "Yet have I left a daughter"—he says it twice. True enough, but not the one he meant. Lear has no idea of Regan's character and wonders why she could have left home; or perhaps this may be only to try and persuade himself against his better judgment that she is still the daughter he imagined her to be. When she refuses to see him at Gloucester's castle he bursts forth in a temper again (the Duke of Cornwall was not the only one who was "fiery" and "unremovable and fix'd" "in his own course"): but this time he soon calms down and reasons quietly with himself, making excuses for her—until he sees Kent in the stocks again and her actions speak louder than words. Notice that when Regan meets him she addresses him as "Your highness", not as "Father". Lear cannot understand her taking sides with Goneril, and, as when Goneril first opposed him, it is a little time before it dawns on him—"Say, how is that?" Regan is a weaker nature than Goneril, and this led Lear to believe that she was kinder, but she soon shows herself in her true colours now that she has the power. She refuses to accept her father with even one follower. Her words to him in this scene (II. iv) are despicable. She taunts him with being old and gives bitter rejoinders to his pleas. How pitiful when Lear reasons that Goneril must be twice the love of Regan because "Thy fifty yet doth double five and twenty", just as he thought (or affected to think) that his daughters would love him because he had given them a third of his kingdom—"What can you say to draw a third more opulent than your sisters?" But life is not so simple as that: it would be very easy to judge a person's character if it were. So Lear rushes out into the rising storm, completely disillusioned about Regan, as well as Goneril.

Lear's rising madness is not due to the loss of his train, nor, primarily, to the storm, but to his realisation that he has placed false trust in two worthless daughters and lost the one who really loved him.

Lear is verging on madness at the end of Act II, Sc. iv. The terrors of the storm and contact with another madman (as he supposes) turn his wits completely.

The doctor's treatment restores him to a harmless lunacy: reunion with Cordelia restores his mind, not to its former strength, but to a simple serenity—"Pray you now, forget and forgive, I am old and foolish". Yet every now and again the old Lear returns.

> He that parts us shall bring a brand from heaven,
> And fire us hence like foxes. Wipe thine eyes;
> The good-years shall devour them, flesh and fell,
> Ere they shall make us weep: we'll see 'em starve first.

Nothing shall separate him from Cordelia now. He will not weep now he is with her, even though it be in prison.

Nothing shall separate him save death, that is. And then he loses all that was dear to him in life. "Now she's gone for ever! Cordelia, Cordelia! stay a little." However, he did what he could, and with a touch of pride tells that he "kill'd the slave that was a-hanging thee"—notwithstanding his years. The adventures of Kent and the fate of his other two daughters make no impression whatsoever on him. He can give his mind only to Cordelia.

Lear's last words as he looks on Cordelia's lips are capable of more than one interpretation.

> Do you see this? Look on her, look, her lips,
> Look there, look there!

It is a happy thought that he imagines he sees signs of life on Cordelia's lips, and dies in hope, as a few minutes previously he had fancied for a moment that she was about to speak, "What is't thou say'st?"

But he dies at the end of the play a better man than he was at the beginning. His sufferings and experiences (meeting the poor unfortunates in his kingdom) have made him think of people worse off than himself, for whom suffering is a common lot in life. They have made him exercise more self-control, and endure things when he is in no position to alter them. In authority, a monarch in his palace, he had never had occasion to do either, but now he has had to expose himself "to feel what wretches feel", he reproaches himself that he has "ta'en too little care of this". Professor A. C. Bradley calls this "The Redemption of Lear". For the sake of convenience the development of Lear's madness and the stages in his "redemption" are set out separately.

Gloucester and Edgar similarly through their sufferings learn to sympathise with others.

The Development of Lear's Madness

I. iv.   Either his notion weakens . . .

> O Lear, Lear, Lear!
> Beat at this gate, that let thy folly in,   [*Striking his head.*
> And thy dear judgment out!

I. v.   O, let me not be mad, not mad, sweet heaven!
Keep me in temper: I would not be mad!

II. iv.   *Hysterica passio*, **down.**

O me, my heart, my rising heart! but, down!

O sides, you are too tough;
Will you yet hold?

You heavens, give me that patience, patience I need!

III. ii.   My wits begin to turn.

III. iv.   His wits begin to unsettle.

Thou say'st the king grows mad!

III. vi.   All the power of his wits have given way to his impatience.

Fool. Prithee, nuncle, tell me whether a madman be a gentleman or a yeoman?
Lear. A king, a king!

His wits are gone.

The trial scene shows Lear's mind quite deranged.

IV. ii.   A father, and a gracious aged man
          . . . . .have you madded.

IV. iv.   As mad as the vex'd sea; singing aloud;
Crown'd with rank fumiter . . .

IV. vi.   I am cut to the brains.

O, matter and impertinency mix'd!
Reason in madness!

IV. vii.   Still, still, far wide!

And, to deal plainly,
I fear I am not in my perfect mind.

The great rage,
You see, is kill'd in him.

The Stages in Lear's " Redemption "

II. iv. After his usual fury upon opposition—"Vengeance! plague! death! confusion!" (as in Act I) Lear calms down. He cannot, however, restrain his temper for long—

My breath and blood!
Fiery? the fiery duke? Tell the hot duke that—

But after this short outburst he tries to find excuses for Regan and Cornwall, "No, but not yet: may be he is not well". Then he sees Kent in the stocks and rages again, but not in such a fury.

Lear does not lash out at Regan as he did at Cordelia and Goneril. He closes the discussion with her with a pitiful plea, only four lines of which show sign of temper.

III. ii. He determines to exercise more self-control—"No, I will be the pattern of all patience; I will say nothing".

He thinks of the Fool.

III. iv.   No [I will not punish], I will weep no more ...
.... Pour on; I will endure.

He thinks of Kent and the Fool before himself, and then of all wretched creatures. "O, I have ta'en too little care of this!"

IV. iii. At first a proper sense of "burning shame" prevents his agreeing to see Cordelia.

IV. vii. He realises Cordelia's superiority in character to himself, and acknowledges that she has some cause to do him wrong.

V. iii. Finally, his shame is overcome and her love is the only thing that matters in life. He thinks of what she has done for him, not what he has done for her.

> When thou dost ask me blessing, I'll kneel down,
> And ask of thee forgiveness.

> Upon such sacrifices, my Cordelia,
> The gods themselves throw incense.

When he loses her the shock is too much for him, and he dies too.

Cordelia

I am sure my love's more richer than my tongue.

Cordelia makes a deep impression. Grossly wronged, she goes out of her way to return good for evil. It comes as a surprise to be told that she speaks only just over a hundred lines and appears in only four out of twenty-six scenes. This is in keeping with her character, a retiring nature of few softly spoken words ("Her voice was ever soft and low"). On the stage she is usually cast for a "petite" actress (Lear is able to carry her body).

The idea of flattering her father in order to get something out of him is repugnant to her, as it would be to any right-minded daughter. Similarly she shuts out Burgundy from her life when she sees that his love is nothing away from her dowry.

> Peace be with Burgundy!
> Since that respects of fortune are his love,
> I shall not be his wife.

Few words, but clear and final. She "cannot heave her
heart into her mouth". The more we feel, the less we
speak, usually. Unreal feeling instinctively tries to disguise
itself in words. Her love and her grief are matters for
her heart, not for advertisement.

> It seem'd she was a queen
> Over her passion, who most rebel-like
> Sought to be king o'er her.

And when she feels the tears coming into her eyes, "Away
she started to deal with grief alone". True love and true
grief are generally the more sincere the less demonstrative
they are. We distrust people who wear their heart upon
their sleeve. Cordelia's strong, sincere, quiet reserve had
won admiration at court: Kent's farewell to her is

> The gods to their dear shelter take thee, maid,
> That justly think'st, and hast most rightly said.

After her "going into France" the Fool kept to himself
and "much pined away". Cordelia knows what her
sisters are like and, notwithstanding their glib professions
of love, fears for her father in their care: she would "prefer
him to a better place". Therefore, by means of the
"good Kent" she keeps in touch with things.

Yet Cordelia is not a paragon of virtue that tries our
patience like Chaucer's Grisilde.* She is a real woman who,
by her actions, some might say "imperfections", has a
share in causing the tragedy of *Lear*. Had she humoured
her old father, just to please him, things would have been
different—and (let us face it) there would have been no
play. But the folly of those we love is the hardest thing
to bear in life, and she is astounded at Lear's incredible
folly and, a sincere nature, disgusted at her sisters' false
protestations, and, by intentional contrast, she answers
Lear with a curt one-word answer—"Nothing". She has
something in her of her father's headstrong determination.
She even gives way to pointless exaggeration in order to
hold her ground, saying that when she gets married and
has a husband to love she will be able to love her father
only half as much as before, which is ridiculous. No one
shall be left in any doubt where she stands.

* *The Clerk's Tale.*

> *Lear.* So young, and so untender?
> *Cordelia.* So young, my lord, and true.

She speaks plainly, not submissively, to her sisters, "I know you what you are". The real tragedy of life is the evil that comes from well-meant actions, the acts of those "Who, with best meaning, have incurr'd the worst": blood and terror make only melodrama.

When her sense of honesty and propriety is outraged Cordelia can be firm and to the point. But at the same time she is kind, modest and unassuming, very ready to acknowledge the good in others, a complex character, such as we meet in life itself. "O thou good Kent," she says, "how shall I live and work, to match thy goodness?" After the treatment she had received she could hardly have been blamed if she had left her father to fend for himself, but when her father, for whom she was risking her life, tells her that she has cause not to love him, "No cause, no cause" are the two words that come straight from her heart.

In defeat it is not for herself that she minds.

> For thee, oppressed king, am I cast down;
> Myself could else out-frown false fortune's frown.

Then comes a flash of that haughty contempt which we have noticed before, "Shall we not see *these daughters and these sisters*?" and we can imagine the tone in which she says it. These are her last words in the play.

> Thou'lt come no more,
> Never, never, never, never, never!

Cordelia knew the risk when of her own free will she left her new country to come to the aid of her father.

> We are not the first
> Who, with best meaning, have incurr'd the worst.

The sacrifice for which she was prepared shows the meaning of her love. She does not "taste the wages of her virtue". That is tragedy. Virtue would cease to be virtue if it *paid*. Her fate is tragic, indeed, but not depressing, for without her death we should not have realised the strength of her love, the length to which it was prepared to go. Lear had spoken of filial ingratitude. But here we are inspired with admiration and wonder at the heights to which filial love can rise. Love proves itself greater than death, not in theological dogma, but in the life and action of a woman. The death of Cordelia may be tragic in the accepted sense, but the impression of the nobility of her character that the play leaves with us is inspiring. What happens to Cordelia does not matter—all that matters is what she is. The play would have been more tragic if Cordelia had stopped in France and saved her life.

In common with all Shakespeare's heroines (save Juliet, whose mother is against her) Cordelia has no mother. The dramatic effect of this is to throw them on their own resources in moments of stress. Cordelia has no other person on whom she can rely (the dramatic reason for France's return), and this awakens our sympathy for her lonely hand and increases the pathos of her situation. Lonely endeavour in a time of crisis more easily reaches heroic proportions.

Goneril and Regan

Two pernicious daughters.

The theme of the play springs largely from the attitude of these two sisters to their father (see p. 14).

The character of Goneril is stronger, more forthright and practical. "We shall further think of it", says Regan, putting off a decision; "We must do something, and i' the heat", Goneril decides for her. Goneril stands up to her father face to face (I. iv), and when he interrupts her, ignores his outburst and brings her speech to an end as she had meant to. She rides roughshod over him with a "take it or leave it" attitude—"At your choice, sir". Regan shrinks from meeting him and slinks away to Gloucester's house to postpone the meeting; then, when he arrives, pretends to be sick and weary and unable to see him, and when she does meet him she makes weak excuses—to him and to herself.

> I am now from home, and out of that provision
> Which shall be needful for your entertainment.

> This house is little: the old man and his people
> Cannot be well bestowed.

> For his particular, I'll receive him gladly,
> But not one follower.

> O, sir, to wilful men
> The injuries that they themselves procure
> Must be their schoolmasters.

It is plain why Edmund has gone to kill Gloucester, for political reasons, as Regan admits (IV. v. 9-11), but a weaker character than Goneril adds the excuse that could not delude anybody, that it is "in pity of his misery". Goneril always takes the lead over Regan, *e.g.*

> If she sustain him and his hundred knights,
> When I have show'd the unfitness,—

She has more initiative than her sister. Only at the beginning of III. vii does Regan make a suggestion before Goneril. When she says something pleasant—how much she loves her father—she falls back on Goneril's words, and similarly, in unpleasant things, she shows a readiness to take a step further the cruel suggestions made by others. Cornwall says that Kent shall sit in the stocks till noon; she follows this up with, "Till noon! till night, my lord; and all night too". Goneril wonders why Lear needs "five and twenty, ten, or five" followers; "What need one?" adds Regan. When Cornwall has put out one of Gloucester's eyes, it is Regan who says, "One side will mock another; the other too". She not only urges Cornwall to carry his cruelties further, but does it with a sneer, and when she thrusts Gloucester out she adds the taunt that he can "smell his way to Dover". So to her father she says, "I pray you, father, being weak, seem so", and in answer to Lear's "I gave you all", her cruel repartee is, "And in good time you gave it". Goneril is without her sister's sadistic enjoyment of cruelty.

These "dog-hearted daughters" think only of themselves, but Goneril is firmer and more unashamed. Goneril would never have asked Gloucester for his advice on any problem; she would have decided for herself, just as she tells her husband to mind his own business and leave things to her—"Never afflict yourself to know the cause". When her father threatens to reclaim his kingdom, "Do you mark that, my lord?" she says to Albany. She is out for power, and if her father stands in her way his fate is of no importance. She welcomes Cornwall's death, as an easier pathway to supreme power. She poisons Regan and plans to have her own husband murdered—by someone else—to avoid complications which stand in the way of her desires. Regan's hypocrisy and bitter taunts make her the more contemptible. With a false air of sympathy for Gloucester's troubles she tells him to forget them and give his attention to hers (her final words in II. i). It is she who first tells Gloucester to shut his doors on her own father, because "He is attended with a desperate train"—an excuse which deceives no one. (Cornwall gives a reason a little nearer the truth.) Yet this is the daughter who would not, so Lear said, "Bandy hasty words", and "oppose the bolt against my coming in". Because she is a less forceful character Lear imagined that Regan was more "kind and comfortable". In the first scene of the play he addresses Goneril as "Our eldest born", but Regan as "Our *dearest* Regan". He was just as mistaken in Regan as he was in Cordelia. The action of the play springs from Lear's misunderstanding of his daughters.

Finally, when Goneril cannot face things out, she has the fearlessness to commit suicide. She is the more formidable, Regan the more detestable.

Coleridge notes the atmosphere clinging around Goneril and Regan and how in their presence "not a sentiment, not an image, which can give pleasure on its own account is admitted". On the contrary, the most beautiful image in the play is the description of Cordelia when she read Kent's letters (the Gentleman's fourth speech in IV. iii).

Gloucester

I stumbled when I saw.

Gloucester is a well-intentioned old man, but weak. He does not stand up firmly for right, but submits without much protest to the evil of others and then tries to work against them secretly. He evades a decision and waits to see how things turn out. "Frame the business after your own wisdom", he says to Edmund, "I would unstate myself, to be in a due resolution" (I. ii).

He comes on the stage at the start of the play, and in very bad taste makes pleasantries about Edmund's illegitimacy *in front of him*. Could anything be more inconsiderate or more calculated to make Edmund jealous, and he goes

on to say (obviously because his presence was incon-
venient to him) that Edmund "hath been out nine years,
and away he shall again". Gloucester then is self-
indulgent and heedless of the feelings of others.

Unlike Kent, Gloucester does not utter one word of
protest against Lear's casting off of Cordelia, though, to
be fair, he was present for only the last part of the incident.

"A credulous father!" says Edmund, and he knows how
to employ his cunning to make Gloucester susceptible to
his suggestions, playing particularly upon his superstition.
"These late eclipses in the sun and moon portend no good
to us", believes Gloucester, and Edmund takes care to
impress it on him that Edgar is in league with the
devil.

> Here stood he in the dark, his sharp sword out,
> Mumbling of wicked charms, conjuring the moon
> To stand auspicious mistress.

Towards the end of the play Edgar in turn plays on his
father's superstition to make him believe that he has
fallen down from a cliff when he has fallen only to the
ground.

Gloucester tries to "play safe" in the part he takes in
the political division of the kingdom. He pleads for
Kent—once—with Cornwall, but not strongly, and then
stops behind to say a few comforting words to him—not
knowing that it is Kent, of course (end II. ii). "I would
have all well betwixt you", he says to Lear, but he avoids
declaring himself (II. iv). He draws Cornwall's attention
to the "bleak winds" at the time that Lear rushes out into
the approaching storm, yet without any great ado, but
then goes secretly to succour him. But would he have
done so if it were not good policy? "These injuries the
king now bears will be revenged home; there is part of a
power already footed: we must incline to the king."
Then comes a welcome touch of duty and affection so far
absent. "Though I die for it, as no less is threatened me,
the king my old master must be relieved" (III. iii). He
fails to speak his mind to Cornwall until his double-dealing
has been found out, when his avowal can make his position
no worse.

The sight of a blind man always stirs pity; how much
more should pity be stirred by the sight of a man so cruelly

blinded? But this must not make us forget that Gloucester had only himself to blame for his distress. Edgar sees it at once. "The dark and vicious place where thee he got cost him his eyes". Added to which we may count his folly in believing the son who was a stranger against the son who had always been with him. But Gloucester cannot see his faults (men who can do so are rare). He is conscious of no relationship between the calamities that have befallen him and his character—"As flies to wanton boys, are we to the gods; they kill us for their sport". With Lear he would consider himself "More sinn'd against than sinning".

Suffering improves the character of Gloucester, even as it does that of Lear (see p. 21). His character too is "redeemed", but not so sharply or clearly, as it is less powerful to start with. His sufferings make him think of the sufferings of others. He tells his old tenant to leave him. "Thy comforts can do me no good at all; *thee they may hurt.*" The thought in his last speech but one in IV. i is identical with that of Lear in III. iv. 28-36. Suffering takes toll of his resistance, mental as well as physical resistance.

> Thou say'st the king grows mad! I'll tell thee, friend,
> I am almost mad myself: I had a son,
> Now outlaw'd from my blood; he sought my life,
> But lately, very late: I loved him, friend,
> No father his son dearer: true to tell thee,
> The grief hath crazed my wits.

While he shows no evidence of anything which could be called madness, it is obvious that he has felt a terrific strain. His language here is exaggerated, however, for in his last speech in the play (IV. vi) he wishes he were mad like the king, so that he would be less conscious of his injuries. When he found out that his poor guide was his wronged son "his flaw'd heart . . . burst smilingly". Lear's end came through shock, but owing to losing—not gaining —his wronged daughter (though see p. 21). Like Lear, Gloucester dies a better man at the end of the play than he was at the beginning.

The student should here note again the parallelism in the fortunes of Lear and Gloucester set out at the end of the section on Source of Plot and Treatment, pp. 11-13.

Edmund

Despite thy victor sword and fire-new fortune,
Thy valour and thy heart,—thou art a traitor;
False to thy gods, thy brother, and thy father.

While the above words are a true description of Edmund, it must yet be allowed that his treatment by his father serves to account for his conduct and by so much to extenuate his sin. In the first few minutes of the play Gloucester introduces him to Kent as an illegitimate son whom it is convenient to have out of the way (see pp. 28-29), an awkward consequence of his infatuation for a fair woman. No wonder that Edmund is embittered, particularly against the brother who stands in the line of true inheritance "by order of law". He cannot help his birth and goes through life with a sense of inferiority for which he is not responsible. The wonder would be if he were not embittered by his father's pleasantries at his cost.

Edmund knows that he is a clever and capable young man, however much he may be despised, and as circumstances have denied him pride in his position, so he takes pride in carrying through a cunning scheme to improve his future. "Let me, if not by birth, have lands by wit." Examples of Edmund's cunning are given at the end of this character-study. Cunning is the dominant feature of his character. He judged the temperament of his father well to delude him so successfully, considering that he had not seen him for nine years. He plays his hand with extreme self-confidence, with no henchmen to assist him (such as Conrade and Borachio in *Much Ado about Nothing*).

In political affairs he quite deceives Cornwall ("Natures of such deep trust we shall much need"), and his father, by betrayal of whom he wins the family estate at one stroke.

This seems a fair deserving, and must draw me
That which my father loses,—no less than all:
The younger rises when the old doth fall.

He is thoroughly selfish and wastes no time on his father's misery. Cornwall says that "the revenges we are bound to take upon your traitorous father are not fit for your beholding", but we can believe that he could have stood looking at these too. In love he does not declare himself for Goneril or Regan, but cunningly lets each wonder

where she stands, and plays one off against the other while
he makes up his mind.

> To both these sisters have I sworn my love,
> Each jealous of the other, as the stung
> Are of the adder.   Which of them shall I take?
> Both? one? or neither?

In battle he is brave and competent.   He leads Regan's
forces and wins the battle; he fights Edgar in single combat,
when "by rule of knighthood" he need not, and on this
account, according to Goneril, he is "not vanquish'd, but
cozen'd and beguiled".   But he is not going to be used as
a tool.   Goneril encourages him to kill Albany
(IV. ii. 19-21), but Edmund considers this too great a risk
and decides to leave it to her (V. i. 60-63).   It would appear
that he is hoping to marry Goneril, as the readiest way to
supreme power, since she was the elder sister.   He decides
to have Cordelia and Lear disposed of as possible rivals,
since Albany intends them mercy and might abdicate in
favour of either.   This would leave the kingdom open to
him if Albany was out of the way and he married Goneril.
His cunning and deceit come out again, for Cordelia is to
be killed to make it look as if she "fordid herself" in her
despair.   When Goneril is dead and he is dying, however,
and the deaths of Lear and Cordelia can do neither of them
any good, he makes it known that they are under sentence
of death.   "Some good I mean to do, despite of mine own
nature".   But too late to save Cordelia.

Every man likes to mean something to somebody.   It
is an instinct deep down in human nature.   *Somebody*
loved the outcast for whose existence his father thought it
necessary to apologise.   As he looks back on life his
greatest pleasure is the thought that two princesses have
struggled with one another for his love.

> Yet Edmund was beloved:
> The one the other poison'd for my sake,
> And after slew herself.

Edmund's Cunning

He pretends to hide Edgar's supposed letter—so that
Gloucester will want to see it all the more.

He makes excuses for Edgar in order to disarm Gloucester's suspicion.

He predisposes Edgar to accept his suggestions by mentioning eclipses, etc. Even if Edgar does not believe in astrology he may wonder if there is any connection, and subconsciously be more prepared to regard a sudden shock as something to be expected.

He tells Edgar to forbear his father's presence, which (since he was with his father for two hours the night before) his father will interpret as the result of a guilty conscience— or of being found out, and so his absence will rouse Gloucester's suspicion of Edgar further (I. ii).

His picture of Edgar "mumbling of wicked charms, conjuring the moon" and of himself appealing to "the revenging gods" is calculated to influence a superstitious mind.

When Regan asks if Edgar was not one of Lear's "riotous knights" (and Gloucester, curiously enough, does not know), Edmund is quick to say that he was "of that consort".—Is it true? (II. i).

He tells Regan and Cornwall of Gloucester's aid to the king and the letter Gloucester has received about an invasion, and he is an out and out hypocrite in pretending that he does not *want* to tell Cornwall of Gloucester's disloyalty but his duty forces him to do so (III. iii and v).

He pretends to be in love with Goneril and Regan— "To both these sisters have I sworn my love" (V. i).

Secretly he arranges for the death of Lear and Cordelia (V. i and iii).

Kent

Having more man than wit about me.

Cornwall hits off Kent pretty well when he says,

This is some fellow,
Who, having been praised for bluntness, doth affect
A saucy roughness, and constrains the garb
Quite from his nature.

Kent's outspokenness is to be admired in I. i, "be Kent unmannerly when Lear is mad", but his lack of self-restraint in picking a quarrel with Oswald in II. ii is the worst service he could have done his master, and Kent thereby diminishes Lear's chances of a more kindly reception by Regan. He is well-meaning but tactless. Under the circumstances it would have been much better to forget

Oswald's sauce to Lear on a previous occasion. Just like Cordelia, Kent plays into the hands of Goneril and Regan. Again, he has only himself to blame that he is put in the stocks. "The best of me is diligence", he says, and his devotion risks death still to serve the master who has banished him. He seeks service with Lear in a characteristic way (I. iv), replying to his questions with blunt one-word answers, being careful to add a touch of compliment which is all the more effective coming from one so outspoken—"You have that in your countenance which I would fain call master". (Such a touch he failed to add when he spoke to Cornwall, which turned his plainness into rudeness.)

On the worst night that anyone can remember Kent will not leave his master out on the heath. He returns good for evil by going out of his way to share his misfortune and soften his adversity. He looks after Lear on the heath with a sturdy masculine tenderness—"Now, good my lord, lie here and rest awhile". When the Fool is frightened he takes his hand in his strong grip assuringly. His dogged faithfulness reminds one of Adam in *As You Like It*, except that he is a person of more importance in the state. Cordelia, whose opinion is worth having, honours him highly—"O thou good Kent, how shall I live and work, to match thy goodness". Kent's devotion in following "his enemy king" reinforces the impression that Lear is a great king past his prime. He knows that Lear is not himself, or he could not have honoured him so.

When all is said and done, Kent is an arrant snob, with an aristocratic contempt for the servant class. He may have disliked Oswald, but no credit to Kent to despise him *because he is a servant*, a "beggarly, three-suited, hundred-pound . . . worsted-stocking knave", and it was poor acting on his part into the bargain.

At the end of the play when everyone is attending to duel, death, poison and suicide, Kent is the only one who remembers Lear. "Is he not here?" he asks in surprise. "Great thing of us forgot! Speak, Edmund, where's the king, and where's Cordelia?" bursts out Albany. And so Kent may be said to have saved his master's life—for the short time remaining to him.

Kent's age is, of course, more than forty-eight (I. iv).
He obviously gave this age to stand more chance of entry
into Lear's service. He tells Cornwall that he is too old
to learn, and in his last speech in the play says that he has a
journey "shortly to go" (obviously he means the journey
to death), but it says much for his physique that he could
pass as forty-eight. Edgar refers to Kent's strong arms
(V. iii. 212), and apparently the night out in the storm had
no bad after-effects on him, and he gives the whole impression of a man of a sturdy breed.

Edgar

A brother noble,
Whose nature is so far from doing harms,
That he suspects none.

By his flight Edgar plays into his brother's hands. He
draws suspicion on himself and leaves Edmund without a
rival. It is incomprehensible how Edgar could have fled
without seeking an interview with Gloucester, or desiring
more positive proof from a brother whom, so far as we
know, he had not seen for nine years. Perhaps the reason
is that he "is so far from doing harms, that he suspects
none", "on whose foolish honesty my practices ride easy".
His brother hustles him and he loses his head in an
emergency. Although he is not superstitious ("Do you
busy yourself with that?"), he is as credulous as his father
in other things. Certainly he is no coward, and is eager to
take up his sword against Edmund at the end of the play—
and against Oswald also, if that counts for anything.

Notice that Edgar does not treat Edmund as if he were
inferior. "How now, brother Edmund!" is his first
greeting. The taunt that Edmund said Edgar had used
against him, "Thou unpossessing bastard!" would have
been the last Edgar would have wanted to use. He
mentions his bastardy only *after* his evil deeds have been
exposed (V. iii. 171-174).

Edgar is at hand as poor Tom when his father needs
comfort and guidance. He lavishes care and affection
upon him.

At the end of the play Edgar shows more common sense
than at the beginning, and this time keeps his head in an

emergency. When Edmund says that his writ is "on the life of Lear and on Cordelia", Albany says, "Run, run, O, run!" but Edgar sensibly replies, "To who, my lord?— Who has the office? send thy token of reprieve". "Well thought on", says Edmund, "take my sword". Just previously, when the Gentleman comes in "with a bloody knife", shouting "Help, help, O, help", Edgar, in very practical fashion says, "What kind of help?"

It is Edgar who sees the radical connection between Gloucester's self-indulgence and his suffering.

Upon Edgar Albany lays the responsibility of sustaining "the gored state", and we feel that it is in good hands. In addition to possessing fine qualities of character, Edgar is, apparently, good-looking. Edmund acknowledges that his opponent's "outside looks so fair", and Albany (wise after the event, though) thought his "very gait did prophesy a royal nobleness".

Albany

Where I could not be honest,
I never yet was valiant.

Albany is a well-meaning type, married to a devilish wife, who by virtue of her position and her personality naturally takes the lead. He is not so weak as he is often presented. The very fact that Goneril keeps him in ignorance of what is going on shows that she had some concern about the action he would take if he knew. He is not like Cornwall, a willing accomplice of his wife, and the difference between the two dukes introduces contrast, of course. Cornwall is the only character in the play who has no redeeming features in his character.

In the first scene in which he takes any part (I. iv) Albany tells Lear, "My lord, I am guiltless, as I am ignorant of what hath moved you", and starts to make a mild protest to Goneril and warns her that she may "fear too far". Goneril does not enlighten him, but shakes off his enquiries, casually informing him that it does not concern him. He is, however, too submissive in accepting this position, and quietly agrees to wait and see how things turn out—"Well, well, the event". This was his great mistake, for had he taken a more active interest the evil to Lear might have been prevented. One of Lear's knights has noticed that "a great abatement of kindness appears as well in the general dependants *as in the duke himself also* and your daughter". This can have been the result only of Albany's following his wife's lead as the easiest course to take and not his precise intention. He speaks of his "great love" for Goneril, and it must be allowed that any husband of Goneril would not only have needed extraordinary strength of character to make her change her mind after it was made up, but would have wrecked his home life in the process. When Albany next appears (IV. ii) he seems a "changed" man (l. 3), though really he is less changed than woken up. Like Edgar he acts more wisely at the end of the play than at the beginning. He now realises the implication of events, and what they show of his wife's character. His own sincere horror at the cruelty inflicted on Lear and Gloucester shows his real nature. He must fight an invading enemy, but his heart is with the invader. He cannot make up his mind what is best to do and keeps blaming himself (V. i. 3-4), and if he wins the battle he intends mercy to Lear and to Cordelia (V. i. 63-64). After his duty for the state is done he can be very firm with Edmund.

> Sir, by your patience,
> I hold you but a subject of this war,
> Not as a brother.

He asserts his authority, demands Edmund's prisoners (for the safety of whom he may have a fear) and offers to settle his quarrel with Edmund by the sword if necessary. Edmund is a man to be reckoned with, and this shows that Albany, like Edgar, is no coward. He is kindly and considerate too, and when Regan feels unwell he interrupts his challenge to Edmund to arrange for attention to be given her. He receives a beggar kindly and agrees to "o'erlook" his letter.

Goneril had spoken with great contempt of her "mild husband" (IV. ii. 1) and his "milky gentleness" (end of I. iv), but she now finds to her surprise and to her cost that, normally easy-going, he could be roused when wrong was being done.

> Shut your mouth, dame,
> Or with this paper shall I stop it.

Yet at the end of the play Albany has learnt nothing. Instead of using the authority and power of decision of which he was capable to rally "the gored state", he lets go his responsibility and repeats Lear's error at the beginning.

> Friends of my soul, you twain
> Rule in this realm, and the gored state sustain.

The Fool

> But I will tarry; the fool will stay,
> And let the wise man fly.

We are well disposed towards the Fool when he first appears. Lear has not seen him "these two days"; his enquiries show that he has missed him (I. iv), and the reason for his absence is that "Since my young lady's going into France . . . the fool hath much pined away". The Fool's attachment to Cordelia at once recommends him to us.

The Fool of *King Lear* is a fragile, pitiful creature. He has "pined away" when we first set eyes upon him. The storm is too much for his physique, and he goes so far as to pray Lear to go back and "ask his daughters' blessing". "This cold night", he says, "will turn us all to fools and madmen" (III. iv). Lear pities his sufferings (III. ii. 63-68; iv. 26) and Kent offers him his hand as if he were a poor, wilting creature when he runs out of the cave frightened. Apparently the effects of exposure in the storm prove too much for him, as we never hear of him again after III. vi. He must have been numb with cold, for otherwise there would have been no need for Kent to tell him not to stay behind.

It is reading too much into the Fool's last words, "And I'll go to bed at noon", to say that they imply that he is finished. Lear has just said, "We'll go to supper i' the morning", and what more natural than that the Fool should follow this up by saying, "I'll go to bed after I've had supper", that is at noon? The dramatic reason for his departure is, of course, that "poor Tom" now takes the antic interest, and two such in the play would be monotonous and redundant.

The Fool is no mere clown (see pp. 39-40). His sallies have point and purpose. He is a shrewd observer of events,

and many of them (*e.g.* in I. iv) go to show that the real
fool of the play is Lear, who has handed over his kingdom
to two such daughters—"Why, this fellow has banished
two on's daughters, and did the third a blessing against
his will". His remarks to Kent in II. iv imply that he is
on the wrong side.

When Lear's wits are gone, however, it would be cruel to
press his folly upon him any more, even if he could understand it, and then the Fool simply "labours to out-jest his
heart-struck injuries" (III. i. 16-17).

The pathos that clings round the Fool's frailty and
round his dogged fidelity to his master, the figure-head of
a losing cause, makes a grim surround to the wit of his
remarks, very appropriate to the horrible tragedy of *Lear*.
The Fool's wit makes little humour; it is hard to laugh
as we see *King Lear*: rather do we give a saturnine smile
in spite of ourselves.

The student should realise the difference between a
clown and a fool in Elizabethan drama. The clown is an
idiot, not a jester.

The clown is largely a caricature, the fool is a character.

We laugh *at* the clown and *with* the fool. The clown is
a victim of the situation, quite unconscious of the fun that
he is causing, the fool master. The clown is less intelligent
than the average man, the fool more.

The clown is a type, English and localised, almost like a
feature of the countryside. He may come from any class
of society, *e.g.* Justice Shallow, Dogberry, Bottom, William
and Audrey, Gobbo's father: the fool takes his place at
court. The professional fool was, in fact, paid to amuse
the lords and ladies of the land by his wit. He was often
on friendly terms with the family. One is reminded of
Touchstone's loyalty to Celia in *As You Like It*; "He'll
go along o'er the wide world with me", she confidently
asserts. So here the Fool does not follow Lear just for
his wages.

Living on such terms fools were accorded much freedom
of speech. But if they went too far (or their master was
in a bad mood) there was always the whip. Lear twice
threatens his Fool with the whip (I. iv). Thus a fool
needed considerable tact to maintain his position.

The fool in Shakespearean drama is a commentator on the situation; he knows better and judges more shrewdly than the others. He is a kind of embodied intelligence.

A fool was expected to sing (and accompany) snatches of song appropriate to any occasion, and the Fool's songs in *King Lear* are perfectly in keeping with contemporary custom in the houses of the great.

STYLE

Professor Dowden has an excellent summary of the development of Shakespeare's style.

In the earliest plays the language is sometimes as it were a dress put upon the thought—a dress ornamented with superfluous care; the idea is at times hardly sufficient to fill out the language in which it is put; in the middle plays (*Julius Caesar* serves as an example) there seems a perfect balance and equality between the thought and its expression. In the latest plays this balance is disturbed by the preponderance or excess of the ideas over the means of giving them utterance. The sentences are close-packed; there are "rapid and abrupt turnings of thought, so quick that language can hardly follow fast enough; impatient activity of intellect and fancy, which, having once disclosed an idea, cannot wait to work it orderly out"; "the language is sometimes alive with imagery".*

King Lear is typical of the latest plays. Shakespeare often expresses more in a sentence than seems possible. Graphic and figurative language abounds, and the vividness of the imagery is to be noted.

"The verse is as great as the invention", says John Masefield.† "It rises and falls with the passion like music with singing. All the scale of Shakespeare's art is used; the terrible spiritual manner of

> "You sulphurous and thought-executing fires,
> Vaunt-couriers to oak-cleaving thunderbolts."

In a wild, savage play like *King Lear* the imagery is generally compelling rather than beautiful—"My father with his bleeding rings, their precious stones new lost". It is very noticeable how the imagery fits the characters present; there are no pleasant images when Goneril and Regan are on the stage (see p. 28), but when Cordelia returns, "a queen over her passion", to aid her suffering father,

---

* *Shakspere Primer*, p. 37. (See footnote p. 7.)
† *William Shakespeare*, Williams and Norgate.

> Patience and sorrow strove
> Who should express her goodliest. You have seen
> Sunshine and rain at once: her smiles and tears
> Were like a better way: those happy smilets
> That play'd on her ripe lip seem'd not to know
> What guests were in her eyes; which parted thence
> As pearls from diamonds dropp'd.

The beauty of this simile and metaphor, naturally combined in one conception, is all the more striking in a play in which there has been so little beauty of description. Sometimes a metaphor is expressed in a single adjective, as in "*wide-skirted* meads", or "*plighted* cunning" (I. i).

The close-packed, elliptical style of many speeches in *King Lear* is inferior dramatically, as it is difficult to follow the thought at the speed at which the words are spoken, but the *form* of Shakespeare's mature verse is dramatically far superior. His verse is very free, making the dialogue more natural and more adapted to different characters. Many lines are "run-on", that is, the sense of one line is completed in the next and there is no stop at the end of the line; the stronger pauses are placed within the line at different points; many lines have extra unaccented syllables. It would be futile to give examples when all the longer speeches of the main characters are typical of Shakespeare's later style.

In a good play the style naturally reflects the character of the person speaking, and even the same person in two different moods may speak in two different ways. Look at Lear's abrupt and disjointed speeches in anger or in madness, and contrast them with his speeches in the early part of the first scene of the play. In dazed grief at the loss of Cordelia, Lear speaks in monosyllables (V. iii. 258-264). It is in situations like this that Shakespeare is so great. The more we feel, the less we speak, usually. Affected feeling instinctively tries to disguise itself in words. Here is real human grief, not melodrama.

In *King Lear* Shakespeare makes full use of dramatic irony—the difference between the situation as known to the audience and as supposed by the characters of the play (or by some of them). The basis of dramatic irony is ambiguity of meaning. A remark by one character may have a surface meaning for the other characters in the play but an additional significance for the audience. Dramatic irony is very effective on the stage, and examples are therefore listed here.

Lear's division of his kingdom "that future strife may be prevented now" (I. i.).

"Some villain hath done me wrong", says Edgar to Edmund, which Edmund backs up with, "That's my fear".

Lear's reliance on Regan when Goneril has proved false to him—"Yet have I left a daughter"—only too true, but not the daughter he meant (I. iv; see also p. 19); and also his telling Regan, "Thou shalt never have my curse" (II. iv).

Cornwall's reliance on Edmund, "Natures of such deep trust we shall much need" (II. i. 115).

The sketch of Cornwall's character drawn by Gloucester, who was so soon to be the victim of Cornwall's "fiery quality" (his first speech in II. iv).

Gloucester's warning to Edmund, which is to be turned against himself, "There is some strange thing toward, Edmund; pray you, be careful".

In the presence of Edgar (poor Tom) Gloucester says, "Our flesh and blood is grown so vile, my lord, that it doth hate what gets it", meaning Edgar, but really it is Edmund who hates his parent.

Edgar calls the blind Gloucester "father", interpreted by Gloucester as a colloquial address to an old man.

Cordelia tells Kent that she cannot match his goodness, "My life will be too short, and every measure fail me".

The normal line in Shakespeare's plays is a blank verse iambic pentameter. Shakespeare's conventions in the use of verse and prose (those of his time) are not followed continuously in *King Lear*. It is as if the convulsive nature of the play broke through custom and carved its own form. Generally speaking, scenes where the emotions are agitated are in verse, and quieter scenes (or parts of scenes) in prose.

Antithetical dialogue was the fashion at the time that *King Lear* was written. There are fashions in literary style as in everything else. This fashion of speech and writing was set off by John Lyly's *Euphues* (1579) and was known as "Euphuism". Lear reproves Cordelia, "How, how, Cordelia! mend your speech a little, lest it may mar your fortunes". He swears "by the sacred radiance of the sun, the mysteries of Hecate, and the night". Kent goes to "shape his old course in a country new". France takes

> Fairest Cordelia, that art most rich, being poor;
> Most choice, forsaken; and most loved, despised!

(where the antitheses are in a figure of speech known as oxymoron) and ends his speech telling her, "Thou losest here, a better where to find". These examples are from the first scene only, and the student will find others elsewhere in the play.

THE ELIZABETHAN THEATRE AND ITS EFFECT
ON PLAYS

AT the time of Shakespeare there were probably not more than five public theatres in the land, all in London, and they were built according to the design of the inn-yards of the period, which had been found marvellously convenient places for the presentation of plays.

The theatre was circular or octagonal in shape. The main part of the auditorium was the large round pit, open to the sky, in which the poorer people *stood* (the "groundlings"). Encircling this, round the walls, were three balconies, covered on top but not in front (like the "stands" on a football ground), and containing seats. The price of admission to the pit was one penny, equivalent to about one shilling and ninepence nowadays, and balcony seats ranged from twopence to half-a-crown, according to their position. When it was wet the performance was postponed until the next day.

The stage was large, which made it easy to show crowd and battle scenes, and they are thus frequent in Elizabethan drama. It jutted far into the pit; hence it made no difference that people stood at the side of the stage as well as in front. It was without scenery and any but the most meagre properties. The scenery was created in the imagination of the audience by the words of the characters in the play, so as not to obtrude and destroy the illusion of reality. *King Lear,* so much of which happens at night, would be performed in broad daylight. The audience is made aware of the imaginative setting, so different from the actual setting when the play was produced, by little natural touches in the dialogue, *e.g.*

> *Edmund.*   Here stood he *in the dark*, his sharp sword out,
> Mumbling of wicked charms, *conjuring the moon*
> To stand auspicious mistress.
> *Regan.*   Thus out of season, *threading dark-eyed night* (II. i).

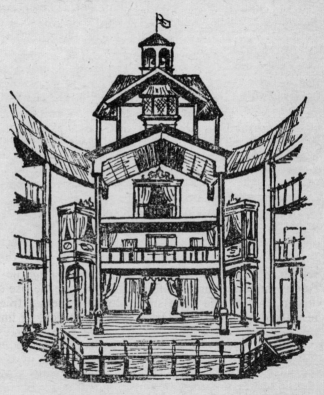

Night-time is often implied without a specific reference, *e.g.* by Kent's inability to see Cordelia's letter and by his saying he will sleep out the time (end II. ii). Similarly the references to the storm help to keep it ever before us (III. i, ii, and iv).

The play went straight on without intervals. Lack of intervals and frequent changes of scene were immaterial when the stage was without scenery, consequently a succession of short scenes, as in Act III, is quite common in

Elizabethan drama. In a modern play with change of scenery the audience would become impatient at the constant delays. There is good reason to believe that Shakespeare's plays took considerably less time than they do to-day. The Prologue to *Romeo and Juliet*, for instance, refers to "the two hours' traffic of our stage".

In the absence of curtains the end of a scene was frequently marked by rhyming lines, as in Act I, Scene i, at Kent's departure, at France's departure, and at the end of the main part of the scene (the part in verse), at the first two of which there are several rhyming couplets, and also at the end or nearly at the end of Scenes ii, iii, and iv. The rhyming couplets in Kent's farewell speech are probably intended to show the end of the episode where he appears and to give his words a clinching epigrammatic effect as well (*cf.* the last two lines of Act III, Scene iii). Remember that Shakespeare did not divide his plays into acts and scenes (see p. 48) and that what seems the end of only a part of a scene as printed in our editions may well have appeared the end of a separate incident to him, as here. In *King Lear*, however, Shakespeare's use of rhyme to end a scene is not so consistent as in many plays, in the same way that his use of verse and prose is not so regular.

Just as the scenery had to be *put into* the play, so had entrances and exits to be arranged as *part of* the play. To-day an actor can get into position before the rise of the curtain, but on the open stage it would seem artificial if he walked on and then started his first speech, or finished the scene and then walked off. Such endings as I. iii, "Prepare for dinner", or v, "Come, boy", clear the stage and at the same time fit in perfectly naturally with the play. It follows that dead bodies always had to be carried off the stage in the action of the play.

It was not unknown for the stage floor to be equipped with a trap-door for the sudden appearance and disappearance of ghosts and spirits, and some theatres had a flying apparatus by which such could descend on the stage with the aid of ropes on runners.

At the back of the stage was a recess "within", and this was curtained and could be shut off when desired. The recess no doubt served for the hovel where the Fool finds Edgar in III. iv.

Above the recess was a balcony, which served for an upper room, castle walls and suchlike scenes. This, too, could be curtained off. Edmund calls Edgar down from the balcony in II. i, "Brother, a word; descend: brother, I say!"

People who wanted to be in the public eye were able to hire stools actually on the stage itself. Payment of one shilling extra entitled them to have their pipes lighted by a page, thus showing to all and sundry that they were in a position to be attended. Such a privilege would be valued by country gentlemen who wanted it to be known that they had come up to town. It was a source of continual annoyance to playwrights that actors "gagged" in order to please these aristocratic playgoers.

Women were not allowed to act by law. Consequently women's parts had to be taken by boys with unbroken voices. Considering the limited emotional range of a boy's voice, imagine a boy's rendering of Lady Macbeth or Cleopatra, or even Goneril! The ban on actresses accounts for the few women's parts in plays of the period, though some were always introduced for the sake of variety. In *King Lear* there are only the three sisters and they were prescribed in Shakespeare's source. It also accounts for the large number of plays where a woman disguises herself as a page boy. It made it much easier for the producer; further, the audience was intrigued by a situation in which a character was pretending to be what he really was! In *The Merchant of Venice* every one of the women disguises herself as a man.

Plays were not acted in period costume, though frequently *some* attempt was made to suggest a period, and the result must often have been a bizarre compromise. Thus all Shakespeare's plays can be said to have been first acted in "modern dress". Although there was no scenery, managers spared no expense on the most lavish of costumes.

On days when the theatre was open a flag was flown from the turret, and when the play was about to begin a trumpet was sounded. The turret of the Globe Theatre housed a big alarum bell, a favourite theatrical effect. This would be the bell that rang out the alarums for the battle and the retreat (V. ii). Perhaps it would lend more impressiveness to Shakespeare's flimsy battle scene.

Teachers will find Brodie's Educational Filmstrip, *The Theatre in Shakespeare's Day*, helpful in presenting the theatre of *King Lear* more vividly.

One must not imagine that it was difficult for Shakespeare to write plays for such a theatre. It would have been difficult for him to write for any other than the one he was used to. What we have never known we never miss.

THE TEXT OF SHAKESPEARE'S PLAYS

FEW readers of Shakespeare realise the difficulties scholars have had to overcome in order to establish accurate texts of the plays. The First Folio (see pp. 6-7) contained thirty-six plays. Other collected editions or Folios were published in the seventeenth century, the Third and Fourth Folios containing seven additional plays, none of which, with the exception of *Pericles*, is now thought to be by Shakespeare. Sixteen of the plays had already been published separately as Quartos before 1623, and in the case of some plays, for example *Hamlet*, more than one Quarto edition exists. Some of these Quartos are almost word for word the same as the texts in the First Folio and were possibly set up from Shakespeare's own manuscript or at least from accurate theatre copies; but others are shortened, inferior versions, possibly "pirated" editions published by some unauthorised person who had access to theatre copies or parts of them, or who had taken down the plays in shorthand while they were being performed. It is thought that the texts of the First Folio were set up from the good Quartos and from good theatre copies. But these texts must all be compared, printers' mistakes and other interference traced, before a reliable text can be arrived at. The first editor to attempt the problem of the text was Nicholas Rowe (1674-1718), who also divided most of the plays into acts and scenes, supplied indications of entrances and exits, and lists of dramatis personæ, which are absent from many of the texts in the Quarto and Folio editions. In *King Lear* he had less to do than in most plays, however, as all the acts and scenes are marked in the First Folio, except Act II, Scenes iii and iv, which are incorporated with Scene ii. Act IV, Scene iii is absent from the First Folio. Rowe's divisions are convenient for reference (like the division of the books of the Bible into chapters and verses) but have no important use in Shakespearean study. They were fitted for the stage of his time, but were unnecessary upon Shakespeare's stage with the barest of scenery.

OUTSTANDING CRITICISM OF *KING LEAR*

CRITICAL material on *King Lear* is inexhaustible, and the student may not know where to turn. Here, therefore, is a selection which may prove helpful for advanced study.

Shakespearean Tragedy. A. C. Bradley. Macmillan. Lectures VII and VIII.

Shakespearian Tragedy. H. B. Charlton. C.U.P. Pp. 189-229.

William Shakespeare. John Masefield. Williams and Norgate. Pp. 186-195.

Shakespeare Criticism. (Selections through the years since the Preface to the First Folio.) Ed. D. Nichol Smith. Humphrey Milford. Pp. 68-78, 232-233, 285-289, 328-331.

NOTES

ACT I. SCENE 1

KING LEAR, an old man past his prime, has made up his
mind to retire from active kingship and hand over his
kingdom in nearly equal parts to his three daughters (his
favourite daughter, Cordelia, having a "more opulent"
third).

On the point of announcing the division he asks his
daughters which of them loves him most, a pitiful piece of
canvassing for flattery, which the two elder daughters
humour, but which is spurned by Cordelia, who "cannot
heave her heart into her mouth" and tells him plainly
that she loves him "according to my bond; nor more
nor less".

Thereupon in a fiery temper Lear casts her off penniless—
"my sometime daughter". An old and loyal nobleman
gets himself banished for interceding for her. One of her
suitors will have none of her without a dowry, but the other,
the King of France, accepts her gladly for what she is
herself.

Lear had intended to live with Cordelia, but now proposes
to stay a month at a time with each of his two elder
daughters, Goneril and Regan. At the end of the scene
Goneril suggests to Regan that they should curb his
authority.

This scene gives the occasion from which the rest of
the main plot springs.

> **more affected,** been fonder of, had more affection for.
> **curiosity,** careful scrutiny.
> **moiety,** share (Fr. "moitié" = half).
> **brazed,** hardened, *i.e.* I can now brazen it out.
> **proper,** handsome.
> **some year,** about a year.
> **in my account,** in my regard, so far as I am concerned.
> **deserving,** *i.e.* to be known better.
> **out,** *i.e.* abroad.
> *Sennet.* A set of notes on a trumpet, usually as a signal of someone's
> approach.
> *Enter . . .* LEAR. In Shakespeare's early plays the main characters
> appeared on the stage at the outset, *e.g.* in the history plays. Later
> on, however, *e.g. Twelfth Night* (1601) onwards, he generally leads

50

up to them in the conversation of minor characters, which is dramatically much more effective. Here the situation is briefly indicated before the main character enters to begin the action of the play. From a practical point of view also it means that the first speeches of the main characters are not disturbed by the entrance of late-comers: by the time they speak the audience has "settled down".

coronet, crown—not necessarily a small one, as is made clear by the stage direction following Lear's speech later in the scene, "This coronet part between you. [*Giving the crown*".

Attend, *i.e.* let them attend.

we. The royal "we".

darker, more secret, *i.e.* than Cordelia's betrothal, for everyone knew that.

> "France and Burgundy,
> Great rivals in our youngest daughter's love,
> Long in our court have made their amorous sojourn,
> And here are to be answer'd."

Perhaps it is no accident that Lear uses this word, speaking of a decision that causes so much darkness and terror in the play. (See also p. 16.)

fast, firm (as in to "hold *fast*").

several, separate, respective.

amorous sojourn. An example of a transferred epithet, common in Elizabethan literature. The princes are amorous, not the sojourn, or they have made their sojourn for an amorous purpose.

both. Actually there are three: the use of the word to indicate more than two was, however, not uncommon in Elizabethan English.

nature, natural feeling.

challenge, lay claim to it—as a person who lays down a challenge at a tournament. See note on "*Throwing down a glove*", p. 93.

space, *i.e.* extent of lands.

found, *i.e.* found love.

these bounds. Lear is pointing to places on the map.

champains rich'd, open country enriched.

wide-skirted, *i.e.* broad—a metaphorical adjective.

prize me, value me, or, perhaps, I value myself.

deed. A metaphor from legal documents.

square of sense, *i.e.* the four senses—sight, hearing, taste and smell.

felicitate, very happy.

More richer. Double comparatives and superlatives are common in Elizabethan English (usually to give emphasis).

hereditary, offspring, lineage (a noun).

validity, value.

milk, *i.e.* dairy pasture-land.

interess'd, interested, concerned.

bond, duty (as a daughter).

nor . . . nor, neither . . . nor (common in Elizabethan English).

Good my lord. A common address at the time (*i.e.* Shakespeare's time), no doubt originating in a desire to emphasise the "goodness" of the person addressed. *Cf.* "dear my lord", V. i. 13.

are. Strictly speaking the verb should be singular, but it is attracted to "duties".

all, altogether, entirely.

plight, plighted troth. *Cf.* "troth plight", in one of Edgar's doggerel verses, III. iv.

Hecate. Goddess of witchcraft and sorcery in classical mythology.

the operation . . . be. Referring to the widespread superstition of Elizabethan times that men's natures and fortunes were influenced by the star under which they were born.

property, sameness, identity.

Hold, regard.

this, *i.e.* this time.

Scythian, of ancient Scythia (a region north of the Black Sea), far enough away in time and place to serve for an example of barbarousness.

he that . . . appetite. Shakespeare is probably thinking of Atreus, who, in classical mythology, had the flesh of the two sons of Thyestes served to their father at a banquet. Thyestes, however, did not "make his generation messes" himself.

sometime, *i.e.* one-time, former.

his wrath, *i.e.* the object of his wrath.

set my rest, throw myself; a metaphor from cards, meaning "stake all I have left".

nursery, care.

give . . . from, *i.e.* take it away from (and give to someone else).

digest, arrange, settle, dispose of.

effects, manifestations (of power).

additions to, attributes of, titles of.

from, *i.e.* away from.

fork, *i.e.* arrow-head.

doom, judgment.

answer my life, let my life answer for.

reverbs, echoes, reverberates.

pawn, pledge.

wage, lay as a wager.

blank, cynosure, bull's eye; metaphor from a target, which had a white mark (Fr. "blanc") in the centre.

Apollo. One of the great gods of classical antiquity, though there is no significance in the choice of this particular god.

strain'd. In the sense "strained to the limit".

power, *i.e.* of carrying out the sentence.

place, *i.e.* title, standing.

Our potency made good, *i.e.* as a proof that we have the power.

diseases, inconveniences; "*dis*-ease" is the opposite of "ease".

Jupiter. See note p. 67.

This shall not be revoked. Lear drives home his sentence by throwing back Kent's own word in his face ("Revoke thy doom").

sith, since.

justly, rightly.

approve, prove to be true. "Your deeds" is the subject, and "your large speeches" the object.

Flourish. A trumpet-call, corresponding to the Sennet on the King's arrival. (See note on "*Sennet*", p. 50.)

Here's France and Burgundy. Gloucester had been sent to fetch them. As commonly in Elizabethan English the names of the countries stand for those of their lords. The verb is singular, either because attracted to the noun next to it, or because the two are thought of as a pair.

Hath. Although the antecedent of "who" is "you", the verb is attracted to "this king", which comes next to it. Many similar instances will be found in the play.

present, *i.e.* immediate.

seeming, *i.e.* really she is nothing.

pieced, *i.e.* into the bargain.

like, please.

owes, owns, possesses.

stranger'd. Elizabethan English was in a much more fluid state than modern English, less "set" in its usage, and it is common to find one part of speech made to serve as another.

makes not up, *i.e.* its mind.

To, *i.e.* as to.

best object, *i.e.* the object of your greatest affection.

argument, subject.

Most best, most dearest. See note on "More richer", p. 51.

dismantle . . . favour. A metaphor from putting away a garment, particularly applicable to some of the elaborate dresses, hoods, ruffs, etc., of contemporary fashion.

monsters, *i.e.* makes it monstrous.

Fall'n, *i.e.* must be fallen.

for I want, because I lack.

dishonour'd, dishonourable.

still-soliciting, always begging.

history, story, account.

regards, "respects" (in Cordelia's next speech).

entire, whole.

Since that. A redundant "that" is often added to conjunctions in Elizabethan English.

choice. In the sense, "having been chosen".

their cold'st neglect, *i.e.* that of Lear and Burgundy.

waterish. Is this in derision of the wine or the weather of Burgundy?

unprized, beyond price, unprizable. *Cf.* "dishonour'd", note above.

unkind, they are unnatural.

benison, blessing.

wash'd, *i.e.* by tears.

professed, full of professions (of love).

bosoms. Implying love and affection.

prefer, recommend (as in "preferment" in the Church).

the want that you have wanted, the lack of fortune that (by your behaviour) you obviously have desired: in other words, "You have got what you asked for".

plighted, involved, *lit.* pleated (hence "unfold"). Indeed, some editions read "plaited", which is a variant of the same word. Another metaphor from a folded garment; *Cf.* note on "dismantle . . . favour", above. It is not the same word as "plight", note p. 52.

Who, those who.

of his time, *i.e.* years of his life.

long-ingrafted. Metaphor from a branch of a tree grafted to another tree. In some editions the reading is "engraffed".

unconstant starts, fickle fits and starts of temper.

hit, agree, "hit it off".

dispositions, tempers, things he is disposed to.

offend, injure—a stronger word then than now.

i' the heat, *i.e.* strike while the iron is hot—lose no time over it. This characteristic of Goneril shows the essential difference between her and Regan.

ACT I. SCENE II

Gloucester's illegitimate son, Edmund (whom we have seen Gloucester acknowledge rather brazenly at the beginning of Scene i) with extreme cunning persuades his father that his legitimate son and heir, Edgar, desires his death so that he can succeed to his property the sooner.

After that, with even more subtle cunning, he persuades his brother, Edgar, that his father is enraged with him and that for his own safety he had better keep out of his father's way.

This takes place the day after Scene i. At the end of Scene i Goneril said that Lear was going away the same night, and here Gloucester says that the King left the night before.

The scene sets the sub-plot in motion. As Lear relies on the promises of two bad daughters and turns against a favourite daughter, so Gloucester relies on the word of a bad son, whom really he does not know, and turns (or is turned) against a good one who has (so far as we know) lived with him all his life.

to thy law . . . bound, *i.e.* to natural law (where the strongest or wiliest wins) instead of to the law of human custom (which keeps down the illegitimate son).

in, subject to.

curiosity, precise or careful custom or law. *Cf.* note p. 50.

deprive, *i.e.* of my inheritance.

moonshines, *i.e.* months.

top, do better than, rise higher than.

to-night, last night. Not as Goneril uses the word at the beginning of her talk with Regan at the end of Sc. i.

subscribed, *i.e.* signed it away (the literal meaning—written underneath), given it up voluntarily.

exhibition, an allowance (as an "exhibition" at a university).

gad, spur of the moment.

Putting up the letter. This, of course, was calculated to make Gloucester want to see it.

o'er-read. o'er-looking. It made little difference in Elizabethan English whether the preposition or adverb came before or after the main verb or noun of a compound word, *e.g.* "my *down*sitting and my *up*rising".

essay or taste, trial or test. Both words have the same meaning.

policy and reverence, *i.e.* policy of reverencing.

of our times. See note on "of his time", p. 54.

idle and fond, useless and foolish.

my closet, my own room.

character, handwriting. It has been said to be strange that Gloucester does not know the handwriting of his own son. It is, however, more likely that Edmund, who has been out of the country for nine years, should know what Edgar's handwriting looks like than Gloucester, who has had no need to receive letters from him.

certain, sure.

where, whereas.

pretence, intention.

Nor is not. In Elizabethan English a double negative intensifies the idea, instead of logically cancelling it.

wind me into him, get to know what he purposes or thinks. The "me" has no force, and is a survival from an old dative, originally signifying "for me".

unstate myself, give up my position or rank.

resolution, certainty.

presently, immediately—the literal meaning.

convey, conduct.

these late . . . moon. There was an eclipse of the moon in September, 1605, and of the sun in the following month. When Guy Fawkes's gunpowder plot was discovered on November 5th, the popular superstitious mind saw a clear connection. This has some bearing on the date of the play (see p. 16).

the wisdom of, *i.e.* our being wise about.

mutinies, insurrections, rebellions (not necessarily only of soldiers).

bias. A metaphor from bowls, a popular Elizabethan game.

disquietly, unquietly.

foppery, foolishness.

disasters. The word has this very derivation, from Lat. "astrum", star. *Cf.* the word "ill-starred".

treachers, traitors (guilty of treachery).

spherical predominance, the period when certain celestial spheres are at their period of greatest influence over human lives. It was a widespread superstition that men's natures and actions were influenced by the stars, indeed, that a man's whole nature was influenced by the star under which he was born.

pat, just at the right time. To "do it pat" is still a colloquial expression.

old, *i.e.* old-fashioned.

cue. Continuing with another figure of speech from the theatre.

Tom o' Bedlam. The name given to mad beggars. "Bedlam" is a corruption of "Bethlehem", from London's big lunatic asylum, dedicated to St. Mary of Bethlehem.   See II. iii. 13-20.

fa, sol, la, mi.   Edgar hums these (tonic sol-fa) notes, perhaps to give the impression that he is humming to himself and not expecting anyone's approach, or perhaps they are suggested by a punning allusion to divisions in another sense, *viz.* trilling notes. On an instrument like a harp it is impossible to play a long note, so the note was said to be "divided" into a succession of shorter notes to give a similar effect.

he, *i.e.* the author of the "prediction".

succeed, follow.

diffidences, occasions of distrust.   The word "diffidence" is derived from Lat. "diffidere", to distrust.

cohorts.   While it can be an easy way out of a difficulty in a Shakespeare text to say that the reading is corrupt, it is obvious from the context that the reading here should be "courts".

sectary astronomical, devotee of astrology.

forbear his presence.   To Gloucester, of course, this will seem evidence of his guilt.

practices, plots.

wit, good sense, brains, cleverness.

ACT I.   SCENE III

Goneril expresses her annoyance at Lear's conduct, and tells her steward, Oswald, to "come slack of former services" to Lear, so as to bring things to a head.

This scene foreshadows the beginning of Lear's troubles in the next.

my gentleman.   Probably Oswald himself.   Goneril is considering the offence as it affects her.

one gross crime or other.   The exaggeration of annoyance.

odds, variance.

slack of former services, *i.e.* to Lear.

question, *i.e.* dispute, which would bring things to a head. *Cf.* what Goneril says l. 26—"That I may speak".

Whose mind . . . one.   See the end of I. i.

Idle, foolish.

authorities, powers residing in authority.

as, instead of.   The sense is, "Old people must be rebuked instead of flattered".

abused, deceived.

occasions, opportunities.

hold, keep, maintain.

ACT I.   SCENE IV

Kent, in disguise, gets service with Lear, and supports his master in a brush with Oswald.

Goneril's humiliation of her father results in an open break. She reduces Lear's hundred followers to fifty, and he threatens to "resume the shape which thou dost think I have cast off for ever". He determines to go to Regan, but Goneril sends Oswald with a letter to her sister acquainting her of what he purposes, especially of her "particular fear".

Lear begins to see how foolish he was in casting off Cordelia and dividing his kingdom between Goneril and Regan. Goneril here shows herself in her true colours, now that she has nothing to lose.

defuse, disguise.

issue, result.

labours, *i.e.* work for him.

dost thou profess, is your profession. Kent affects to take the enquiry in a different sense.

trust, *i.e.* a position of trust.

converse, live.

judgment. Kent probably means in a court of the land (not the Last Judgment).

eat no fish, *i.e.* eat well. (It would not be like Shakespeare to intend the meaning, "Not to be a Catholic".)

Who wouldst thou serve? Notice that Kent addresses Lear as "you" when he answers, and that Lear addresses Kent as "thou". The Elizabethan convention in the use of "thou" and "you", while not absolutely constant, is illustrated in this conversation between Lear and Kent. "Thou" was a sign of familiarity (used by a master to servants and between close friends), "you" was a formal address, customary, for example, from servant to master.

Incidentally, the correct form "whom" (instead of "who") was as much neglected in those days as in these.

curious, one that needs to be told carefully. *Cf.* note on "curiosity", p. 50.

forty-eight. On the stage Kent looks older than this (also see his last words in the play). He is meant to lower his age in order to be considered for employment.

knave, boy (without any derogatory sense). See later in the scene, where Lear calls Kent his "friendly knave".

sirrah. A contemptuous (or familiar, as later in the scene when the Fool so addresses Lear) form of "sir", generally used when speaking to inferiors. The repetition of "you" emphasises Lear's contempt. Obviously he has no love for Oswald *before* this encounter.

So please you, *lit.* so may it please you, the common phraseology of a polite request or apology, but said here in such a way as to imply, "If you please, I do not wish to answer".

clotpoll, blockhead.

roundest, plainest.

entertained, received, as we speak of "entertaining" guests.

as, in which.

rememberest, remindest.

curiosity. See note p. 50.

pretence. See note p. 55.

But where's my fool? This third enquiry shows the high place the Fool held in Lear's estimation. Our interest in him is aroused before he comes on the stage, and when he does appear it is in response to a longing of the audience to see him. We are also favourably disposed to him because he feels the absence of Cordelia.

My lady's father. Not "the king".

base football player. In Shakespeare's day football had no status: it was a rough game played by all and sundry in the town or village street, *e.g.* on an apprentices' half-holiday.

differences, distinctions (*i.e.* between "my lady's father" and "king").

earnest, a pledge, wages in advance to show that Lear really did take him into his service.

coxcomb. The fool's cap was surmounted by a cock's comb. Notice how all the Fool's remarks bear on Lear's situation.

an, if.

smile as the wind sits, *i.e.* make the best of it and take the easiest course, adapt yourself to conditions as they are.

catch cold. Implying by being turned away.

banished, *i.e.* from his affection.

on's, of his. "On" and "of" were readily interchangeable in Elizabethan English, as they are in unlettered speech to-day.

a blessing. Presumably by sending her to a peaceful kingdom with a worth-while husband, but whereas the general sense of the Fool's remarks can be followed, logical sequence is not to be expected of a jester.

nuncle. A more tender and childlike address than "uncle" (perhaps a contraction of "mine uncle").

thy. Notice how the Fool first addresses Lear as "you", but addresses Kent (a servant) as "thou", and then, more familiarly, speaks to Lear of "*thy* daughters". See note on "Who wouldst thou serve?", p. 57.

the whip. The regular punishment of fools in great houses, when their tongues went beyond what their masters considered proper.

must, that must.

out, outside (to his kennel).

brach, bitch (usually of a hound).

gall, *i.e.* bitterness. Is Lear humorously referring to the Fool, or is he brooding over Oswald's treatment of him?

owest. See note p. 53.

goest, walkest.

trowest, believest.

Set, *i.e.* stake.

throwest, throwest *for*, *i.e.* wager less than you hope to get.

nothing, nonsense.

unfee'd, one who has not been paid, implying that lawyers give no advice without payment.

nothing . . . nothing. Just what he had said to Cordelia in the first scene.

Prithee. A contraction of "I pray thee".

presently. See note on "present", p. 53. This, of course, is the literal meaning of the word.

here. there. Indicating himself and Lear respectively.

will not let me, *i.e.* be "altogether fool" (because they are fools too). The Fool takes "altogether" in a different sense from that in which Kent intended it.

thou borest thine ass. Like the miller and his son in Æsop's Fable, *The Miller, his Son, and their Ass.*

wit, sense.

myself, *i.e.* a fool.

had ne'er less grace, were never less in favour (because there are so many of them, *i.e.* wise men turned fools). *Cf.* the phrase, "grace and favour".

foppish, foolish. See note on "foppery", p. 55.

bo-peep. A children's game like hide-and-seek, in which one child peeps from hiding and suddenly jumps out crying "Bo!" To "play bo-peep" was a phrase used of evasive politicians.

frontlet, *i.e.* a metaphor for her frown.

shealed peascod, *i.e.* a shelled pod—with the peas taken out.

other. Singular or plural in the reign of Elizabeth I.

safe, *i.e.* sure.

late, lately.

put it on, support, encourage.

allowance, approval.

tender of, care for.

weal, welfare.

hedge-sparrow. A cuckoo's favourite choice of nest in which to lay her eggs. Shakespeare is very accurate in his natural history.

it head. "It" was sometimes used as a neuter possessive, but not so commonly as "his".

So . . . darkling. The Fool's remarks often *seem* nonsense, but really have bitter point. The extinguishing of the candle is obviously a reference to Lear's giving up his kingdom. "Darkling" = in the dark.

fraught, filled, furnished.

dispositions. See note p. 54.

the cart draws the horse, *i.e.* things are back to front—the daughter leading the father.

Whoop, Jug! I love thee. This snatch of a song or saying is meant to turn off the sting of what he has just said. "Jug" is a term of endearment.

notion, mind.

lethargied. See note on "stranger'd", p. 53.

would, *i.e.* should like to. Lear would sooner learn that he is a shadow, and then this situation would not be real.

Which. Antecedent "shadow". The Fool is adding to his previous remark.

admiration, wonder.

disorder'd, disorderly.

debosh'd, debauched.

graced, gracious. *Cf.* note on "had ne'er less grace", above.

depend, *i.e.* be your dependants.

besort, sort with, befit.

the sea-monster, the whale, though probably Shakespeare had no actual monster in mind.

kite. A term of reproach, the kite being a bird of prey.

parts, qualities.

worships, honours.

an engine, *i.e.* the rack.

my people. He wants his "people" to be summoned.

It may be so, my lord. Lear is too much upset to pay any attention to Albany.

thwart disnatured, perverse unnatural. See note on "nature", p. 51.

cadent, falling.

fret, wear away.

benefits, *i.e.* what she does to benefit her child.

Within a fortnight. This is sometimes taken as evidence that Lear has been with Goneril a fortnight. It may equally well refer to the future—Goneril has given instructions that he is to be allowed a fortnight in which to get rid of half his train.

untented, incurable, *lit.* unable to be probed by a tent (pad of lint).

fond. See note p. 55.

Beweep, *i.e.* if you beweep.

comfortable, full of comfort.

knave. The word here undoubtedly has a derogatory sense, not the meaning at the beginning of this scene (note p. 57).

At point, in readiness, on the alert.

buzz, whisper.

in mercy, at his mercy.

still, always—the usual meaning in Shakespeare. *Cf.* "still-soliciting", note p. 53.

taken, *i.e.* captured by them.

his heart, *i.e.* his intention of "resuming" his "shape".

full, in full, fully.

my particular fear, *i.e.* that Lear will "resume" his "shape".

compact, make it hold together better.

attask'd, taken to task.

event, issue, result. Albany is content to wait and see how things turn out. His attitude is, "Do not let us try to cross the bridge until we come to it".

ACT I.   SCENE V

Lear makes swift arrangements to leave Goneril's palace and go to Regan, with his train.

He has a fear that his treatment by Goneril is beginning to affect his mind.

Gloucester. If we expect consistency in every detail, this must be the town, since Lear could have had no knowledge that Regan intended to visit the Duke of Gloucester; indeed, she had, as yet, no idea of it herself, and Lear was surprised when he arrived at her palace and found her gone from home. Shakespeare, however, was never very careful about little details of time and place.

out of, *i.e.* as a result of reading its contents.

't, *i.e.* his brains referred to collectively.

kibes, chilblains.

prithee. See note p. 59.

wit, sense, "brains". See note p. 56.

slipshod, shod in loose slippers (because he has "kibes")—the literal, not the metaphorical, meaning. The implication is, of course, that Lear has no brains.

kindly. The Fool is punning on the meaning "after her kind". *Cf.* note on "unkind", p. 53.

crab, *i.e.* crab-apple.

forget my nature, *i.e.* and be cruel (instead of "kind").

the seven stars. A cluster of small stars called the Pleiades.

't, *i.e.* his kingdom. The idea of "resuming" his kingdom is in his mind once more.

temper, a proper blend of feelings, mentally balanced, not letting one's self-control get out of hand. This is the proper meaning of a word which is now used as if it meant only "*bad* temper".

REVISION QUESTIONS ON ACT I

1. What difference between the characters of Goneril and Regan do you notice *by the end of the first scene*?

2. Do you think that Cordelia was churlish, or at least unsympathetic, in failing to humour her old father, or do you consider that she was right to be firm for a principle that he would not understand?

3. Comment on the conduct of Goneril and Lear in the breach between them.

4. What, in general, is the point of the Fool's sallies in Scenes iv and v? Give examples.

ACT II. SCENE I

Even so soon after Lear's division of the kingdom it is whispered that war is likely between the Dukes of Albany and Cornwall.

Edmund stages a scene with Edgar which makes his father think that Edgar is a treacherous son, and causes Edgar to imagine that danger threatens him and he must run away. Gloucester promises to "work the means" to make Edmund his heir.

Regan and the Duke of Cornwall visit Gloucester at night at short notice, and Cornwall promises his support in apprehending Edgar. Regan bids Gloucester "lay comforts to his bosom" concerning his faithless son and give attention to the business upon which she and her husband have come, mentioning "differences" between Goneril and Lear.

The two plots of the play join in this scene.

Save thee. A contraction of "God save thee".

ear-kissing, *i.e.* whispered closely.

arguments. See note p. 53.

toward, in a state of preparation, at hand.

take. See note p. 60.

queasy, ticklish, difficult.

briefness, speed.

descend. See p. 47.

Upon his party, on his side. Edmund asks Edgar whether he has not spoken against one side or the other, giving Edgar the impression of danger all round. He speaks quickly so as to fluster him. Edgar flees before he has had time to consider the supposed dangers properly.

Advise yourself, consider. This verb is often reflexive in Elizabethan English; *cf.* Fr. "s'aviser".

cunning, stratagem.

Yield . . . here! Torches, torches! These words, of course, are shouted out, so that Gloucester will come: Edmund had arranged that he should be watching, when he spoke with him earlier in the day (I. ii), and he was at hand, if not actually watching.

conjuring, invoking. Edgar's "mumbling of wicked charms" and "conjuring the moon" would predispose Gloucester's superstitious mind against Edgar (see Gloucester's last speech in I. ii).

this way. Of course, Edmund points the opposite way to the one by which Edgar left.

But that. See note on "Since that", p. 53.

in fine, finally, in conclusion.

loathly, loathingly.

fell motion, cruel attack. "Motion" was the technical term for the attack in fencing, a popular sport in Elizabethan England.

prepared, *i.e.* kept at the ready.

unprovided, *i.e.* unprovided with defence, unguarded—Edmund's sword was not "prepared".

best, *i.e.* in the best way, thoroughly.

gasted, frightened, terrified. The word still survives in "aghast".

found—dispatch, once he is found—we will hasten (to deal with him).

arch, chief, "master". Now used only in compounds, *e.g.* archbishop.

pight, determined, *lit.* fixed.

curst, bitter and abusive.

discover him, show him up, *lit. un*cover him.

reposal, reposing. People repose no trust, etc., in you, and so would not believe you against my word.

character. See note p. 55. Notice how cunningly Edmund predisposes Gloucester's mind again. Edgar, he says, called him an "unpossessing bastard". (Gloucester would immediately think, "Let Edmund have his inheritance".) Edgar said that he would be unsuspected, "Though thou didst produce my very character", which was exactly what Edmund had done (and Gloucester would not be so inclined to question the authenticity of the letter). If he considered events the letter would not seem so isolated.

practice. See note p. 56.

make a dullard of the world, set the world down as dull.

they not thought, they (the people in the world) did not think.

pregnant, ready.

Strong. In the sense of "firm", "determined".

fasten'd. Means the same as "Strong", above. *Cf.* note on "fast", p. 51.

got, begot.

Tucket. Like "*Sennet*" (note p. 50), a set of notes on a trumpet as a sign of someone's approach.

natural. From the context it is obvious that Gloucester is not referring to Edmund's illegitimacy, but to his natural feelings as a son towards his father.

capable, *i.e.* capable of legally inheriting.

he was of that consort. Edmund cannot lose this opportunity of discrediting Edgar. (Was it true?) "Consort" = company.

though he were ill affected, if he was evilly disposed.

expense, expending.

bewray, show, "discover".

make . . . please, do what you like, and you have my authority for it.

doth. The two subjects are allied in one idea.

threading. Metaphor from threading a needle, implying going through with difficulty.

Occasions, affairs.

poise, weight.

which. The antecedent is understood to be the letters.

from, away from.

several, *i.e.* Lear's messenger (Kent) and Goneril's (Oswald). See note p. 51.

Lay comforts to your bosom. See p. 28.

use, application (of your counsel).

ACT II. SCENE II

Kent (Lear's messenger) meets Oswald (Goneril's messenger) in the early morning at Gloucester's castle, where both have been instructed to follow Regan for her reply. Kent rails at Oswald and ultimately draws his sword and, as he is afraid to fight, beats him with his hands. Oswald's shouts bring Edmund, Cornwall and others rushing in, and Kent gets put in the stocks for his pains.

Gloucester regrets the insult to the King in "stocking" his messenger, but Cornwall and Regan are adamant.

In the stocks Kent longs for daylight so that he can read a letter that he has received from Cordelia. He is "weary and o'er-watch'd", however, and falls asleep.

severally, separately, *i.e.* from opposite sides of the stage. See note p. 51.

dawning. Of the day after the night of the previous scene.

pinfold, pound (whence there would be no escape).

I know thee not. Yet Kent had tripped him up a day or two before (I. iv). Does Oswald really forget Kent, or does he pretend not to know him in view of the reception Kent had given him at Goneril's palace? Remember that it is still night—"Yet the moon shines".

knave. Used in the modern sense (as in note p. 60), not that of the note p. 57.

broken meats. *i.e.* bits and pieces of meat (such as a menial would have to eat).

three-suited. A regular allowance for a servant was three suits a year.

hundred-pound. Again implying a servant—possessed only of £100. Kent here is a poor actor, for a man with £100 in Shakespeare's time was comparatively well off (see p. 15).

worsted-stocking, *i.e.* the sort worn by poor people. Rich people wore silk stockings.

lily-livered, cowardly. The liver was supposed to be the seat of courage.

action-taking, *i.e.* action at law.

glass-gazing, *i.e.* in the mirror.

superserviceable, serving in a fawning way; over-anxious to please, without a sense of independence.

one-trunk-inheriting, possessing only one trunk (*i.e.* all he has can go in one box).

addition. See note p. 52.

varlet, rascal.

sop o' the moonshine. This probably refers to a recipe for cooking eggs in oil, called "eggs in moonshine". In other words, Kent says, "I will beat you up".

cullionly, of low degree, base.

barber-monger, one who often patronises the barber, *i.e.* a fop.

Vanity. A common character in the pre-Shakespearean morality plays (in which the characters took the names of moral qualities, such as Vanity). "Puppet" implies contempt.

carbonado, slash. A metaphor from the preparation of a steak of meat for broiling or grilling by slashing it with a knife.

come your ways, come on.

neat, prim.

With you. Answering Edmund's question—"The matter (argument) is with you".

goodman boy. A term of contempt.

an. See note p. 58.

flesh ye. As we say, "Give you your first taste of blood".

disclaims in, disowns.

unbolted, unsifted, hence coarse.

wagtail. An emblem of check and impertinence.

sirrah. See note p. 57.

holy cords. Not necessarily of matrimony alone, but of all family relationships. Kent is thinking, of course, of the "cord" between Goneril and Lear. It must be admitted that, even if his loyalty is to be admired, Kent does his master little service by his lack of self-control in this scene.

a-twain, in two.

intrinse, tight.

smooth, fall in with, encourage. (The opposite of "smooth over".)

rebel. Strictly speaking should be "rebels", but see note on "are", p. 51.

Renege, say no (the opposite of "affirm").

halcyon, kingfisher. Referring to the old wives' tale that if the dead body of a kingfisher were hung up, its beak would always point into the wind.

epileptic. As is seen from the next line, now he is safe from Kent, Oswald is smirking at him.

as, as if.

Sarum, Salisbury.

Camelot. The legendary city of King Arthur's court. Several places in the south-west claim to be the site of Camelot, but Camelot exists beyond the frontiers of history and geography in the timeless realm of romance. Oswald's laughter suggests to Kent the cackling of geese, and these two lines obviously refer to some lost story about, or reference to, geese in the Arthurian legends.

likes. See note p. 53.

constrains the garb, forces himself to adopt the manner.

from, different from, away from.

more corrupter. See note on "More richer", p. 51.

ducking, *i.e.* bowing and scraping.

observants, obsequious servants.

that stretch their duties nicely, *i.e.* if you give them an inch they do not take a yard. "Nicely" = precisely, exactly.

aspect, influence (as of the stars).

Phœbus. Roman god of the sun. Kent here mimics the affected style of the court (since Cornwall objects to plain speech).

to entreat, by entreating.

his misconstruction, *i.e.* Lear's misconstruction.

conjunct, in league with him.

being down, *i.e.* I being down.

worthied him, got him credit.

attempting, assaulting, setting on.

self-subdued, *i.e.* Oswald did not retaliate because he controlled himself.

fleshment. See note on "flesh ye", p. 64.

Ajax is their fool, *i.e.* Ajax is a fool compared to them. Ajax was a Greek warrior in the Trojan War, and hence Kent is saying that the boastful talk of rogues and cowards like Oswald makes a bold warrior like Ajax look a fool.

Till noon . . . too. Regan has little initiative, but is always ready to carry other people's evil suggestions farther.

colour, *i.e.* **kind.** (Goneril had mentioned Lear's "hundred knights". See the end of I. iv.)

away, *i.e.* along.

answer, answer for.

abused, badly treated.

rubb'd, hindered, deflected. A "rub" was an obstacle on a bowling green that interfered with the course of the bowl. *Cf.* "bias", also a metaphor from the game of bowls, note p. 55.

watch'd, kept awake, as in the New Testament phrase, "Watch and pray". *Cf.* "o'er-watch'd" in Kent's next speech.

out at heels. *Cf.* our phrase "out at elbow".

approve. See note p. 52.

saw, saying, proverb.

Thou . . . sun! *i.e.* out of the cold clammy church into the warm sun, which—contrary to appearances—is a change for the *worse.* Kent is alluding, of course, to Lear's removal from Goneril's home to Regan's.

misery, *i.e.* miserable people—abstract for concrete, as often in Elizabethan English.

shall . . . state. Apparently Kent is drowsy and the sentence is incomplete. The general sense seems to be, "She shall find time to deliver us from this monstrous state".

Losses, misfortunes, calamities. Probably general in sense, and not referring to Lear's loss of authority.

vantage, the opportunity.

turn thy wheel! Fortune's wheel represented the uncertainty of human fortune, for the goddess of Fortune was *blind,* and thus it was sheer chance that determined whether a man came high or low on her wheel as she turned it.

ACT II. SCENE III

"Proclaim'd" far and wide, Edgar decides to escape the hunt by disguising himself as a "Bedlam beggar".

This scene, a soliloquy,

1. Gives necessary information to the audience, so that when Edgar meets Lear on the heath the situation is realised at once.

2. Makes an impression of the flight of time between Kent's being put in the stocks and his discovery there by Lear later in the day.

proclaim'd, *i.e.* as a criminal. Gloucester had said (II. i), "I will proclaim it".

free, *i.e.* open.

That, in which.

attend, wait for.

bethought, minded.

most poorest. See note on "More richer", p. 51.

penury. See note on "misery", above.

elf, tangle, because the tangling of hair was supposed to be one of the tricks of elves.

presented, *i.e.* open.

Bedlam beggars. See note on "Tom o' Bedlam", p. 55.

mortified, *i.e.* deadened (by use) to the pain.

object, appearance.

low, *i.e.* poor, lowly.

pelting, paltry.

bans, curses.

Turlygod. The name under which Bedlam beggars commonly went.

ACT II. SCENE IV

Having followed after Regan from her home to Gloucester's castle, the first thing Lear finds there is Kent in the stocks outside. He cannot believe that Regan and Cornwall could have imposed this indignity, and goes inside to find out what is amiss.

But Regan and Cornwall refuse to see him, and send a message by Gloucester to say so. Lear sends Gloucester to them again more importunately, and this time they come. Kent is set free, but Lear now has more important concerns to attend to.

Regan tells Lear to return to Goneril, who, however, soon arrives in person. It takes a long time for it to dawn on Lear that Regan as well as Goneril is set against him. He ultimately realises that neither of these daughters will give him a home with his followers. And so he dashes off into a gathering storm, and Regan and Cornwall tell Gloucester to "shut up his doors" and come inside.

Lear tries to be patient, but it is not in his nature and he goes out in a pitiful fury. As his troubles increase he feels that they are more than his mind will bear.

cruel. Punning on "crewel" (worsted), a material commonly used for garters.

over-lusty, too strong or lively.

nether-stocks, stockings—another pun.

Jupiter. Juno. Respectively king and queen of the Roman gods.

respect, consideration, considered judgment.

Resolve me, let me know, inform me. *Cf.* "resolution", note p. 55.

modest, moderate, *i.e.* as quickly as reasonably possible.

commend, deliver.

post, messenger. Fresh horses were kept at "posts" at regular intervals along a road; messengers rode more swiftly on relays of fresh horses. *Cf.* "post-haste".

intermission, interruption (of my business).

meiny, train, retinue.

man than wit, manhood than good sense.

drew, *i.e. I* drew.

Winter . . . way. "Winter" stands for Lear's troubles. "Fly" may refer to Regan's "flight" from her father's approach, or the Fool may simply mean the situation in general. The Fool's remarks are cast in a humorous vein, but go to the point cleverly.

bags, *i.e.* money-bags. (Lear had dispensed with his.)

dolours. Punning on "dollars".

tell, count.

mother. *Hysterica passio.* The popular and the medical term for hysteria.

this daughter. Notice that, with the dawning realisation of what Regan's treatment of Kent means, Lear cannot pronounce the name of his "dearest Regan".

chance, chances it that.

i' the winter, *i.e.* inferring that Lear has fallen on wintry days and so his followers are deserting him. It is not that he has dismissed half his train as Goneril demanded.

when a great . . . hill, *i.e.* when Lear's fortunes are running downhill. All the Fool's remarks here emphasise the way of the world in forgetting a man when his fortunes fail.

I would have none but knaves follow it. The Fool himself does not follow it.

sir, man.

the wise man, *i.e.* wise for his own safety.

perdy, *lit.* by God (Fr. "par Dieu").

Deny, refuse.

fetches, excuses, pretexts. *Cf.* our word "far-fetched". Note Lear's pun on the word two lines lower.

still. See note p. 60.

office, duty.

more headier, more impetuous.

remotion, removal (from home). *Cf.* "remove", l. 4 of this scene.

Cry. The Fool takes up the word from the last line of Lear's long speech.

nuncle. See note p. 58.

cockney, silly, affected woman.

knapped, rapped.

coxcombs, heads. It is the Fool speaking. See note p. 58.

naught, evil, wicked.

like a vulture. Elizabethan literature is full of classical allusion and Shakespeare may have in mind the story of Prometheus, whose liver was devoured by a vulture while he was chained to a rock.

she to, *i.e.* she would be likely to.

this, *i.e.* his kneeling.

house, *i.e.* family—any family, family relationships.

Most serpent-like. Lear was to find that this applied more to Regan than to Goneril. Goneril was more direct, Regan more serpent-like.

top, head.

young bones, *i.e.* unborn child. *Cf.* Lear's curse on Goneril in I. iv.

taking, bewitching.

You fen-suck'd fogs. *Cf.* Lear's imprecation upon Goneril in his last speech in I. iv.

tender-hefted, *lit.* tender-handled ("heft" is an earlier form of "haft"). The idea is that tenderness is with her, or follows her.

to cut off my train. Later Regan says, "What need one?"

To bandy hasty words. See later:—

> "*Lear.* I gave you all—
> "*Regan.*   And in good time you gave it."

to oppose the bolt. "Shut up your doors."

offices, duties.

bond of childhood. This was how Cordelia said that she loved him (I. i).

Effects. See note p. 52.

Tucket. See note p. 63.

whose easy-borrow'd . . . follows, *i.e.* Oswald gets his pride from his mistress.

varlet. See note p. 64.

Who comes here? It would seem that Lear did not hear Regan say that Goneril was expected, or at any rate, give any attention to her words. He was, no doubt, more concerned about who put his man in the stocks.

Allow, approve of. *Cf.* note on "allowance", p. 59.

if yourselves are old. Charles Lamb's impression of this passage is worth quoting.

> "On the stage we see nothing but corporal infirmities and weakness, the impotence of rage; while we read it, we see not Lear, but we are Lear,—we are in his mind, we are sustained by a grandeur which baffles the malice of daughters and storms; in the aberrations of his reason we discover a mighty irregular power of reasoning, immethodized from the ordinary purposes of life, but exerting its powers, as the wind blows where it listeth, at will upon the corruptions and abuses of mankind. What have looks, or tones, to do with the sublime identification of his age with that of the *heavens themselves*, when . . . he reminds them that "they themselves are old"? What gesture shall we appropriate to this? What has the voice or the eye to do with such things? But the play is beyond all art, as the tamperings with it shew."

from. See note p. 63.

entertainment, reception. See note on "entertained", p. 57.

squire-like, like a knight in training.

sumpter, drudge (*lit.* pack-horse).

the thunder-bearer, *i.e.* Jove, another name for Jupiter. See note on "Jupiter", p. 67.

Is this well spoken? *i.e.* do you mean it?

sith, since.

slack, neglect, come slack in their services.

control, rebuke.

notice, recognition.

depositories, *i.e.* Lear had deposited his power with them.

well-favour'd, good-looking. *Cf. Genesis*, xxix. 17 (Authorised Version).

superfluous, *i.e.* possessed of more than nature strictly needs.
flaws, bits.
Or ere, before.
bestow'd, accommodated.
his particular, his own person, himself.
The injuries . . . schoolmasters, *i.e.* they must learn from bitter experience.
incense, incite.
abused, deceived.   Not the same sense as in note p. 66.

REVISION QUESTIONS ON ACT II

1. In what ways was Kent's service of little value to Lear? Do you think that he deserved being put in the stocks?

2. Do you consider that Edmund's deception of Gloucester and Edgar in Acts I and II is too easy to be credible? Give reasons, of course.

3. Comment on the conduct and manner of Regan and Lear in the breach between them at the end of this Act.

ACT III.   SCENE I

Kent asks a Gentleman to go to Dover, there to meet with Cordelia and France, who have secretly landed with an army, and to tell her of Lear's "unnatural and be-madding sorrow". But first they will find the King, who is wandering on the heath in a violent thunderstorm.

This scene is to give information to the audience, information obviously conveyed to Kent in the letter he had received from Cordelia (see his last speech in II. ii). Up to now Goneril and Regan have had everything their own way. This scene gives the first hint of opposition.

The scene also gives a change of atmosphere, a rest after the tension of the previous scene between the King in a wild rage (II. iv) and his frenzied defiance of the elements when wandering the heath in the storm (III. ii). This emphasises the frenzy in III. ii, as otherwise the audience could not keep at this level of feeling for so long. A quiet little scene in between at the same time sets it off by contrast and relieves it.

main, mainland.
cub-drawn, *i.e.* her cubs have sucked all her milk, and therefore on a normal night she would seek nourishment.

None but the fool. It was he who had said, "I will tarry; the fool will stay".

upon the warrant of my note, on the strength of what I know about you.

dear, important.

that their great stars, whose great stars (fortunes) are. For "stars" see note on "spherical predominance", p. 55.

seem. This word bears the emphasis.

speculations Intelligent, observers communicating intelligence (information). *Cf.* the "Intelligence Service" today.

snuffs and packings, quarrels and plottings. To "snuff" (or sniff) is a sign of annoyance.

Or, *i.e.* or perhaps it is owing to. Kent's sentence is unfinished—he is in a hurry.

hard rein. Metaphor from managing a horse.

furnishings, outward signs.

power, army.

scatter'd, *i.e.* its resources are "scatter'd", divided between two dukes, instead of presenting a united front.

have secret feet, have secretly landed.

at point. See note p. 60.

to, as to.

on my credit you dare build, *i.e.* you credit what I say.

just, true, correct. *Cf.* "justly", note p. 52.

plain, complain.

blood, *i.e.* good family.

I will talk further with you. Not unnaturally the Gentleman is unwilling to take a stranger's words on trust.

fear, doubt.

fellow, companion, chance acquaintance.

Fie on. An expression of displeasure or disgust.

to effect, in their effect.

the king. Notice that to Kent Lear is still "the king".

pain, effort or trouble be.

I'll, *i.e.* I'll go.

ACT III. SCENE II

Kent finds Lear defying the elements on the heath. They battle against him as if they were in league with his daughters. The Fool is the only one who stays by his master in his extremity. Lear feels that his "wits begin to turn". Kent persuades him to go to a hovel hard by.

cocks, *i.e.* weathercocks.

thought-executing, swift as thought.

Vaunt-couriers, forerunners.

nature's moulds, *i.e.* the moulds in which the forms of nature are cast.

germens, seeds, germs.

spill, kill, destroy.

court holy-water. A proverbial phrase for "fair words".

Nor rain . . . daughters. See note on "if yourselves are old", p. 69.
tax, charge.
unkindness, unnaturalness. See note on "unkind", p. 53.
subscription, obedience. See note on "subscribed", p. 54.
battles, battalions.
The man . . . wake. The Fool's seemingly superficial nonsense generally has pertinent application to Lear's troubles. The best explanation of these four lines is by Furness.

"A man who prefers or cherishes a mean member in place of a vital one shall suffer enduring pain where others would suffer merely a twinge. Lear had preferred Regan and Goneril to Cordelia."

For there . . . glass. Furness goes on:—

"This is the Fool's way of diverting attention after he has said something a little too pointed; the idea of a very pretty woman making faces in a looking-glass raises a smile."

As it happens Lear is much too occupied with his own thoughts to pay any attention to the Fool.
a wise man and a fool. The Fool does not specify which is which. *Cf.* II. iv.

> "But I will tarry; the fool will stay,
>   And let the wise man fly:
> The knave turns fool that runs away;
>   The fool no knave, perdy."

Alas, sir, are you here? Notice that Kent forgets to "Holla" the Gentleman when he finds Lear, which he enjoined upon both of them at the end of the previous scene.
Gallow, terrify.
pother. Another (and stronger) form of "bother".
simular, *i.e.* appearing to be but not really (virtuous), giving a false appearance.
caitiff, despicable wretch.
practised on, plotted against. *Cf.* the noun, note p. 56.
continents, *i.e.* that which contains you.
summoners, *lit.* law officers warning people to appear in court.
demanding, asking. Evidently, after leaving the Gentleman in Sc. i, Kent had gone back to Gloucester's house to see if Lear had changed his mind and decided to return there as the storm was so bad.
Denied. See note p. 68.
and a little. This redundant "and" is common in old ballads and seems to imply emphasis, *e.g. only* a little. This song is a variation of the one sung by the Clown in *Twelfth Night*.
brave, fine.
I'll speak . . . go. This is most unlike Shakespeare. The last speech may be a "gag" by an actor, which has crept into the play. It is not in the Quartos (see p. 48).
are their tailors' tutors, *i.e.* tell their tailors how to make their clothes—decide their fashions for themselves.
Nor cutpurses come not. See note on "Nor is not", p. 55. Cutpurses stole purses by cutting them from the girdle from which they were hung.

to throngs, *i.e.* in crowds.
Albion. Britain—referring to the white cliffs of Dover (Lat.
"albus" = white).
going, walking.
Merlin. The wizard of the court of King Arthur.

ACT III. SCENE III

Gloucester tells Edmund in confidence that he is going
to relieve the King secretly, and also that he has received
a letter telling of "a power already footed" which will
revenge Lear's injuries. Edmund at once decides to tell
Cornwall and turn this news to his own advantage.

Here the Lear plot and the Gloucester plot come more
closely together. Gloucester secretly associates himself
with Lear's party and Edmund is with Cornwall.

Like Scene i (of this Act) this little scene where two men
talk quietly together contrasts with the scenes immediately
before and after it, with Lear's ravings in Scene ii and his
complete madness in Scene iv, as the storm rides in fury
in both.

When I desired . . . house. *Cf.* Gloucester's last speech in II. iv,
and the reply of Regan and of Cornwall.
There's a division between the dukes. Edmund had heard this from
Curan, II. i.
closet. See note p. 55.
home, thoroughly, as far as possible.
power. See note p. 71. Kent is not the only one with this information.
charity, kindness (as in I *Corinthians*, xiii).
toward. See note p. 62.
pray you, be careful. Notice the intense dramatic irony of this
caution. See pp. 41-42.
forbid, forbidden (by Regan and Cornwall).
deserving, deed to get me a reward, by which I may deserve
something.

ACT III. SCENE IV

In wild weather on the heath Lear meets with Edgar
(disguised as a madman), and the mental and physical
strain he has been through, together with Edgar's assumed
madness, turns his wits.

Gloucester finds the King (as he had purposed in Sc. iii),
with the Fool and Kent, who alone refuse to desert him,

and he leads him away to find shelter. Lear will not leave Edgar, and he goes along too.

Now the two plots are running together, Edgar helping (unwittingly) to drive the King mad, and Gloucester giving him aid.

i' the mouth, *i.e.* by a blow in the mouth.

When the mind's free, *i.e.* when one has nothing on one's mind.

as, as if.

home. See note p. 73.

Pour on. He is addressing the storm.

would, which would.

You houseless poverty. Lear begins his address to poor homeless people here, but seeing that the Fool hangs back when told to go in the hovel first, he breaks off to tell him a second time.

loop'd, full of holes, *lit.* loopholes. "Window'd" gives the same idea.

superflux, superfluity. *Cf.* "superfluous", note p. 70.

just. See note on "justly", p. 52.

Fathom and half. The amount of rain that has fallen suggests to the "spirit" that he is at sea taking soundings.

Through the sharp . . . wind. This and the next line, which occurs also in *The Taming of the Shrew* (Induction, 1. 10), are no doubt lines from old ballads or songs. The line is repeated farther on in the scene.

ratsbane, rat poison; like knives and halters, to encourage him to commit suicide.

five wits. A common phrase, matching the five senses.

do de. Suggesting his shivering.

star-blasting. See note on "spherical predominance", p. 55.

taking. See note p. 68. Here the noun.

charity. See note p. 73. It does not mean, "Give poor Tom some money".

and there. He is pretending to catch the foul fiend, whom he imagines to appear in different places.

pendulous, overhanging.

thus little mercy on their flesh. Looking at Edgar's scanty rags.

pelican. A water-bird fabled to tear open her breast to feed her young with her blood. Hence young pelicans were held up as an example of greedy children.

Pillicock. A term of endearment, *e.g.* my pretty darling.

that curled my hair, *i.e.* who was something of a fop.

wore gloves in my cap. As a sign of the "favours" of his mistress.

out-paramoured, had more paramours than.

the Turk. Referring to Turkish harems.

suum, mun, ha, no, nonny. Suggesting the sound of the wind.

Dolphin. An old form of "Dauphin". No doubt the line comes from some old ballad on the French wars.

sessa! An exclamation which may mean "Stop!" or "Never mind!" *i.e.* let the cold wind "trot by", you cannot do anything about it.

owest. Here used in its modern meaning, not as in the note p. 53.

worm, *i.e.* silk-worm.

cat, *i.e.* the civet-cat, a small African animal, whose glands supplied civet, a strong perfume.

unaccommodated, uncovered.

naughty. A much stronger word than now. See note on "naught", p. 68.

lecher, debauched, lustful man.

a walking fire, *i.e.* Gloucester with a torch.

the web and the pin, cataract of the eye, the "pin" being the bright speck and the "web" the film over it.

creature, *i.e.* any creature.

Saint Withold. Saint Vitalis, invoked to give protection against nightmare. These lines are an incantation against it.

old, wold, down.

nine-fold, nine familiar spirits.

plight, *i.e.* not to harm anyone. See note on "plight", p. 52.

aroint thee, away with thee.

wall-newt, lizard.

water, *i.e.* water-newt.

sallets, salads.

ditch-dog, *i.e.* dead dog thrown into a ditch.

mantle, *i.e.* the scum on the surface.

tithing, district—originally a district with ten householders. The phrase corresponds to "from parish to parish".

three suits. See note on "three-suited", p. 64.

deer, animals (of any kind).

Smulkin, *i.e.* his "follower".

is a gentleman. In answer to Gloucester's question, Edgar, in effect, says, "What better company could he have than the prince of darkness?"

gets. See note on "got", p. 63.

is. "Fire and food" are thought of as one creature-comfort.

the house, *i.e.* provided by Gloucester.

Theban. Implying a wise man, Thebes being a city celebrated in the myths of Ancient Greece. So with "Athenian", in Lear's last speech in the scene.

prevent. In its literal meaning of "go (or come) before", forestall.

He said it would be thus. Though when he said it in Act I, Sc. i Gloucester was not present.

blood, *i.e.* family (and as an outlaw his son would be unable to claim his inheritance). See note p. 71.

crazed, shattered.

cry you mercy, *lit.* I cry to you for mercy, a regular Elizabethan way of asking anyone's pardon.

soothe, humour.

Child. In old ballads a title for the son of a knight.

word, password (presumably the password by which to get into the giant's "dark tower"). This refrain lingers on in the fairy-story of *Jack the Giant Killer.*

ACT III. SCENE V

After listening to his father's confidences in Scene iii Edmund has gone straightway to reveal them to the Duke of Cornwall, who promises him the Earldom of Gloucester.

This is the climax of Edmund's fortunes, where he is made Duke of Gloucester in his father's lifetime.

Notice again this little scene where two men talk quietly together, in contrast to the mad ravings of Lear before and after (*cf.* Scenes i and iii). The scene also gives the impression of the flight of time, during which Lear has time to get to the farmhouse, where he appears in Scene vi.

censured, judged (not necessarily unfavourably). Nowadays the word has this meaning of reproof, and "criticised" usually implies it, a cynical commentary on human criticism.
nature. See note p. 51. "Blood" (in Edmund's last speech in the scene) has the same meaning.
fears me, makes me afraid.
himself, *i.e.* Gloucester.
the letter he spoke of. In Sc. iii.
approves, proves. *Cf.* note p. 52.
intelligent. See note on "speculations Intelligent", p. 71.
comforting, aiding.

ACT III. SCENE VI

In the shelter of the farmhouse to which Gloucester had conducted him (see Sc. iv) Lear appears raving mad, and imagines that Goneril and Regan are being tried before him in court. This is a pathetic and, if well acted, a powerful scene.

Gloucester comes with information that he has overheard "a plot of death" upon Lear, and that he has a litter ready in which the King can be driven to Dover.

Frateretto. Supposed to be another fiend.
Nero. Probably a reminiscence (and an incorrect one) of Rabelais's romance, *The Great and Inestimable Chronicles of Gargantua,* where Nero is said to be a fiddler and Trajan an angler. But this need not be pressed. Perhaps no reference to the historical Nero is intended; it may simply be a choice by Shakespeare for the name of a fiend.
innocent, fool.
yeoman. A freehold landowner of some substance, but below the rank of a gentleman.
to, for.
he's a mad . . . before him. Another reference to Lear's folly.
'em, *i.e.* his daughters.

arraign, accuse, charge.

straight, straightway.

she foxes. The fox symbolised meanness and ingratitude. *Cf.* Regan's reproach when Gloucester enters in Sc. vii, "Ingrateful fox!" **he,** *i.e.* the foul fiend.

eyes, *i.e.* looking at you, people to admire you.

Come . . . me. The first line (slightly altered) of *A Songe betwene the Quenes Majestie and Englande,* by William Birche, 1558, the year of the coronation of Queen Elizabeth I. England starts by seeking Elizabeth as Queen. "Bourn" = brook, burn.

Hopdance. Supposed to be another fiend.

white, *i.e.* fresh.

black angel. As opposed to the "*white* herring".

their evidence, *i.e.* the evidence against them.

Bench, *i.e.* sit on the judge's bench.

Sleepest . . . harm. A few lines from another ballad. The blast of his "minikin mouth" will be on his shepherd's pipe, of course. "Minikin" = pretty little, "kin" being a diminutive. If sheep eat corn in the ear it swells up inside them and can kill them.

Cry you mercy. See note p. 75.

I took you for a joint-stool. A proverbial expression. A "joint-stool" was a stool made of parts joined together.

store, material.

Bless thy five wits! Edgar here forgets his part and is overcome with sheer compassion, as he himself realises in his next speech. For "five wits" see note p. 74.

That you . . . retain? "I can be patient" (II. iv), "I will be the pattern of all patience" (III. ii).

The little dogs. A very pathetic touch that Lear should imagine that even the least of the creatures he loved should have turned against him.

brach. See note p. 58.

lym, bloodhound, or lime-hound, so called from the leash (leam) with which it was held in.

Or bobtail tike or trundle-tail, either cur with its tail "bobbed" (cut short) or dog with a curly tail. *Cf.* note on "Or . . . or", p. 89.

Do, de, de, de. See note on "do de", p. 74.

Sessa! See note p. 74.

horn, *i.e.* drinking-horn.

entertain, engage, take into my service. *Cf.* note on "entertained", p. 57.

Persian attire. Probably some topical allusion. Though there are difficulties for us in Shakespeare's plays, we may be sure that they were not difficulties for his audiences.

And I'll go to bed at noon. These are the last words of the Fool in the play (see p. 38), and he leaves it 16 lines farther on.

Stand in assured loss, are assuredly lost.

conduct, guidance, escort.

balm'd, cured.

sinews, nerves.

Stand in hard cure, are bound to be hard to cure. *Cf.* "Stand in assured loss", above.

our woes, woes such as we have ourselves.
sufferance, suffering.
o'erskip. See note on "o'er-read. o'er-looking", p. 55.
portable, bearable.
high noises, *i.e.* noises in high places, that mark important events.
bewray. See note p. 63.
In thy just proof, in true proof of you.
repeals, recalls.
reconciles, *i.e.* with your former companions, in your former position.
What will hap more, whatever else happens.

ACT III. SCENE VII

Cornwall bids Goneril go to her husband and tell him to make speedy preparation as "the army of France is landed".

He sends some of his servants to "seek out the traitor Gloucester", and when he is brought, after questioning him, puts out his eyes, to Regan's heartless comments. A servant rebels against the act, however, and stands up to him, and he is wounded.

Regan and Cornwall turn Gloucester out of his own house, but not before he has heard (from the lips of Regan) that it is Edmund who has betrayed him, and he realises therefore that Edgar has been "abused".

In the previous scene Lear was reduced to his lowest extremity by the cruelty of his daughters, and here it is Gloucester, through the cunning of his son. The parallelism between the two plots is further emphasised.

In this scene the character of Regan appears at its very worst.

Notice the regularity of the structure of Act III, alternately scenes charged with feeling contrasted against ordinary conversational scenes (see also pp. 73 and 76). The feelings of the audience are worked up to such a pitch that a rest comes as a relief. If the emotional pitch were not lowered the audience would be feeling frustrated—they would be longing for a change that did not come, and further, the high-pitched scenes would cease to have the same effect. So the emotional pitch of Scenes ii, iv, vi until Gloucester re-enters and vii is high, and of Scenes i, iii, v and the last 30 lines of vi is low. The division in the middle of vi is unimportant, for Shakespeare was accustomed to write his plays without separate numbered scenes (see p. 48).

Post . . . husband. This is spoken to Goneril. For "post", see note p. 67. Here the word is a verb, however.

this letter. The letter about which Gloucester spoke to Edmund in Sc. iii and which Edmund handed to Cornwall in Sc. v.

bound, ready, prepared.

the duke, where you are going, *i.e.* the duke of Albany.

festinate, speedy.

to, for.

my lord of Gloucester. Edmund has now won all he set out for.

where's the king? Had Oswald been sent to despatch him? Gloucester had "o'erheard a plot of death upon him".

My lord of Gloucester. Oswald's use of the title to mean the old earl emphasises Edmund's quick rise in fortune.

questrists, searchers.

lords dependants, *i.e.* members of Lear's train.

pass, *i.e.* pass sentence.

do a courtesy to our wrath. In which case our wrath would act as it pleased.

Ingrateful fox! See note on "she foxes", p. 77.

corky, shrivelled (with age), like cork.

Bind him, I say. Evidently the servants had hesitated.

To pluck me by the beard. A gross insult.

quicken, come to life. *Cf.* "the quick and the dead".

favours, face, features.

simple-answer'd, simple and to the point in your answers. Some editions read "simple answerer".

guessingly, tentatively.

tied . . . course. Bear and bull baiting (where the animal was tied to a stake while the dogs "baited" it) were popular Elizabethan sports.

anointed. At his coronation.

buoy'd up, risen.

stelled, starry.

holp, helped, *i.e.* called on them to do so.

subscribed, allowed, condoned. See note p. 54.

I'd shake it. See note on "To pluck me by the beard", above.

villain, serf. Not used in the same sense as when Regan calls Gloucester a "treacherous villain".

quit, requite.

overture, disclosure, revelation—made it over to us.

abused. See note p. 66.

old, usual, natural, the one to which everyone has grown accustomed.

the Bedlam, *i.e.* Edgar.

Allows itself to, lets him do.

flax and whites of eggs. White of eggs on flax was a common treatment for wounds at this (Shakespeare's) time.

REVISION QUESTIONS ON ACT III

1. "I will be the pattern of all patience." Give examples of Lear's efforts to be patient in Acts II and III.

2. What other new aspect of Lear's character is revealed in Act III? Show how it is revealed.

3. How does Shakespeare achieve the effect of intense pathos in the storm scenes?

4. Discuss the effect of the scraps of song in the play.

5. Comment on the structure of this Act, scene by scene.

Act IV.   Scene i

Edgar meets Gloucester, and leads him on his way to Dover.

Gloucester is helped in his misery by his outcast son, as Lear comes to be later by his outcast daughter.

known, *i.e.* by myself.

contemn'd, held in contempt.

dejected, cast down (the literal meaning)—in fortune, not merely in spirits.

Stand still in. See note on "Stand in assured loss", p. 77.

esperance, hope.

lives not in fear. Because a man can have no fear of worse when his fortunes are at their lowest ebb.

laughter, *i.e.* a happier state of affairs.

Owes nothing to, is not in debt to—the modern meaning of "owes", not that on p. 53 (or 58). He can be blown only to better things.

poorly led, *i.e.* led by a poor man.

But, except.

mutations, changes of fortune.

Life . . . age, *i.e.* man would not want to grow old.

stumbled, *i.e.* metaphorically.

Our means . . . commodities, our faculties give us a sense of *false* security, and our sheer defects prove our advantages (by making us careful).

abused, deceived (the usual meaning in Elizabethan English—not that on p. 66).

I' the last . . . friends with him. See the last part of Act III, Sc. iv.

should this be, *i.e.* came this about.

play fool to sorrow. As he is going to do to Gloucester, keep up the deception of who he really is.

or rather do thy pleasure. Gloucester realises that he has no authority now. *Cf.* "Do it for ancient love", 4 lines above.

Above the rest, most important of all.

daub it, *i.e.* keep up the disguise ("play fool to sorrow").

Five fiends. The last three were named by Edgar in III. iv, and Hobbididance ("Hopdance") in III. vi.

mopping and mowing, making faces (the two words mean the same). The phrase was borrowed by Christina Rossetti in her *Goblin Market*

to, *i.e.* to be submissive to.

superfluous. See note p. 70, and *cf.* "superflux", note p. 74.

slaves, makes a slave of, enslaves (the established order of things), *i.e.* treats it with contempt, considers only his own pleasure.

ACT IV. SCENE II

Accompanied by Edmund, Goneril has arrived outside her palace, surprised that Albany has not come to meet her. Before Edmund goes back she shows him clear signs of affection, and gives a hint that if he "dare venture in his own behalf" he may well become her husband.

On Albany's entrance he rounds on Goneril about her treatment of her father, but Goneril dismisses his protests as those of a weak "milk-liver'd man".

A messenger comes with news that Cornwall has died from his wound, and thus Albany hears of the cruel treatment of Gloucester (III. vii). The news is double-edged for Goneril, with good and bad possibilities.

From this scene onwards the fortunes of Goneril and Regan are on the decline, with Goneril's husband clearly sympathetic to the other side. Further, we have the first evidence of a rift between Goneril and Regan. The whispered differences between the dukes hitherto have been political (II. i and iii).

our. The royal plural. *Cf.* note on "we", p. 51.
Not met us. *Cf.* note on "they not thought", p. 63.
sot, fool.
cowish, cowardly.
an answer, *i.e.* to resist the wrongs.
prove effects, come to be realised.
brother, *i.e.* brother-in-law (Cornwall).
powers. See note p. 71.
favour, *i.e.* a little keepsake.
thy. Whereas at the start of her speech Goneril called Edmund "you", in this more tender passage she addresses him by the more friendly "thy". See note p. 58.
Conceive, think over what it means.
I have been worth the whistle. The emphasis is on "have been", *i.e.* there was a time when you thought it worth-while to come to meet me (see ll. 1-2). The words are in allusion to a proverb that it is a poor dog that is not worth whistling, and Goneril thinks it apparent that she does not appear "worth the whistle" to Albany now.
fear, fear for.
contemns. See note p. 80.
it origin. See note on "it head", p. 59.
border'd certain, contained with certainty.
sliver, strip off down the bark, not by a clean break. "Herself" is the object of this verb.
material, *i.e.* the sap that has given her substance.
deadly use, *i.e.* the use that dead things are put to.

savour but, have a relish only for.

head-lugg'd, pulled by the head.

tame, *i.e.* modify.

Milk-liver'd. *Cf.* "lily-livered", note p. 64.

Fools, *i.e.* and only fools.

noiseless, *i.e.* without the noise of preparation for war.

begins. The subject is "France", and "thy state" the object.

moral, moralising.

thyself. This is the emphatic word. Goneril has given her opinion of *him*, now he will say what he thinks of her.

Proper, real.

deformity, *i.e.* of character. *Lit.* this line means, "deformity proper to the fiend".

Thou. See note on "Who wouldst thou serve?" p. 57.

self-cover'd, *i.e.* having yourself covered (by a monster or a fiend).

Be-monster not thy feature. Do not turn thy outward appearance into that of a monster.

my fitness, fitting for me.

blood, passion. Not quite the same emphasis in meaning as in Edmund's last speech in III. v. See note on "nature", p. 76.

remorse, pity.

bending, turning. The Messenger does not quite know what happened. Such a discrepancy makes the play seem more (not less) real, for a messenger in real life might be without exact details.

This shows . . . venge! He had thought that retribution must follow (ll. 46-50).

One way, *i.e.* that she may appropriate Regan's share of the kingdom.

May, it may happen that. It is not a wish.

pluck Upon my hateful life, may strip my life (of its pleasure), which would then be hateful to me.

back, on the way back.

ACT IV. SCENE III

In the French camp near Dover, Kent learns of the impression his letters have made upon Cordelia. Her sorrow for her father's condition stands out in sharp contrast to the heartlessness of her sisters. It is made more affecting by the beautiful verse in which it is described.

We learn that Lear is in Dover, but that shame forbids his agreeing to see Cordelia.

know you the reason. The dramatic reason is that France's departure awakens our sympathy for Cordelia's lonely hand and increases the pathos of her situation. Shakespeare's heroines are invariably thrown on their own resources in times of stress (see p. 26).

Who. See note on "Who wouldst thou serve?" p. 57.

your letters. See note on "When . . . acquaintance", p. 83.

the queen, *i.e.* Cordelia.

trill'd, trickled.

a better way. Explained by what follows.

believed, *i.e.* believed in.

clamour moisten'd, *i.e.* her clamour (against her sisters) gave way to tears.

It is the stars. *Cf.* Gloucester in I. ii.

conditions, dispositions.

one self, the same (*cf.* self-same).

the king, *i.e.* the King of France.

elbows, thrusts.

casualties, hazards.

dear. See note p. 71.

When . . . acquaintance. If this is the same gentleman whom Kent sent to Cordelia (III. i) he would already have found out who Kent was by showing the ring that Kent gave him. Further, Kent gave him no letters—it was a verbal message. Shakespeare, however never bothered much about little inconsistencies like this.

Act IV. Scene iv

Cordelia, who appears for the first time since she was roughly cast out by her father (I. i), is seen anxious to meet him and she sends in search of him (whom, in spite of all, she calls a "good man").

News is brought that the British forces are appearing, and Cordelia states that she is prepared for them.

fumiter, fumitory (in Shakespeare's time a herb with a great reputation in medicine). A summer weed, it grows "rank" in dry fields. It has thin, much divided leaves, and grows to a height of about 2 ft.

burdocks. Docks with a bur or prickly head. Some editions read "hor-docks".

cuckoo-flowers, *i.e.* flowers that come with the cuckoo, *e.g.* cowslip or buttercup.

Darnel. A coarse grass weed growing plentifully in cornfields, and very troublesome, since when young it cannot easily be distinguished from the corn. It is the same as the "Tares" of the Authorised Version (*Matthew*, xiii. 28-30).

"The servants said unto him, Wilt thou then that we go and gather them up? But he said, Nay; lest while ye gather up the tares, ye root up also the wheat with them. Let both grow together until the harvest: and in the time of harvest I will say to the reapers, Gather ye together first the tares, and bind them in bundles to burn them: but gather the wheat into my barn."

idle, *i.e.* doing no good; the opposite of "sustaining".

century, body of men, not *literally* a hundred (far fewer would be needed to search even a large open field of Elizabethan times): or perhaps merely "sentry"—the word was not infrequently used with this meaning, but as "a Gentleman with Attendants" is sent to look for Lear (Sc. vi) the meaning is probably the former.

our. Cordelia speaks as a queen. *Cf.* note p. 81.

can, is able to do.

helps, cures.
simples, medicinal herbs.
anguish, pain (physical, as well as mental).
virtues, powers (Lat. "virtus").
Spring, spring up (out of the earth watered by her tears).
aidant and remediate, helping and remedial.
wants, lacks.
important, inportunate.
blown, puffed up. These lines would help to soften an English audience to the idea of French troops successfully crossing the Channel and fighting in their land. (France was our hereditary enemy in Shakespeare's day.)

Act IV.　Scene v

Oswald has arrived at Gloucester's castle with a letter from Goneril to Edmund (see IV. ii. 18-21), but Edmund has gone to despatch Gloucester—because the sight of him moves all hearts against us".

Regan suspects the contents of Goneril's letter and asks Oswald to let her unseal it, but he firmly, though politely, declines. She tells Oswald plainly that now her lord is dead Edmund is more "convenient" for her hand than Goneril's, and bids him tell his mistress so.

Oswald goes after Edmund at once, in spite of an invitation from Regan to delay. He says that if he meets with Gloucester he will be only too glad to "show what party I do follow".

In this scene we see that Regan, like Goneril, has no affection for her sister. Both sisters have been in alliance merely to serve their own ends, and when those ends differ they have no scruples and are prepared to sacrifice each other.

Notice the contrast with the previous scene. There Cordelia's interest was centred on her father. Regan's interest here is occupied with her own selfish desires.

brother. See note p. 81. Here Albany is meant.
nighted, benighted (owing to his blindness).
Belike, perhaps.
Madam, I had rather. Goneril had justly called Oswald a "trusty servant".
œillades, loving glances.
of her bosom, in her confidence. Oswald certainly was: Goneril had no hesitation in making her overtures of love to Edmund in his presence (IV. ii. 14-24). Nor does he betray the confidence that she reposed in him in the slightest.

gather, *i.e.* infer.
when your mistress ... from you. Regan knew that he would tell her.
call her wisdom to her, come to her senses, act wisely. Notice that the idiom is reversed in this expression—bring her senses to her.

Act IV. Scene vi

This scene falls into three distinct parts.

1. Edgar (as "poor Tom", see IV. i) leads Gloucester to the supposed edge of a cliff, and when he throws himself down on flat ground persuades him, in the character of a peasant beneath Dover cliff, that he has jumped down the fearful cliff and been miraculously preserved from death by the gods. (Shakespeare's Cliff at Dover takes its name from Edgar's description in this scene.) This episode can easily become farce in the hands of a poor actor, but Shakespeare brings support to the reality of the "cliff" to Gloucester by his beautiful poetry in describing it.

2. Lear, fantastically dressed with wild flowers, meets Gloucester, and the two victims of plot and sub-plot are thus on the stage together. The Gentleman sent by Cordelia to find Lear (Sc. iv) here comes upon him, and Edgar learns from him that a battle is imminent.

3. As those ordered by Cordelia to bring Lear before her have been successful in finding him, so Oswald, ordered by Regan to slay Gloucester if he should chance upon him, is likewise successful in finding him. He is, however, unable to carry out his command, as Edgar interposes and kills him. Before he dies Oswald implores Edgar to give the letters about him to "Edmund, Earl of Gloucester". Thus Gloucester and Edgar have Edmund's treachery brought home to them at one dramatic stroke.

Edgar opens a letter to Edmund. It is from Goneril (see Scenes ii and v), inviting him to kill Albany and take his place as her husband. He keeps the letter to show to the Duke.

that same hill. See Gloucester's last speech in IV. i.
anguish. See note p. 84.
thou speak'st ... didst. Edgar has not forgotten his part. He is preparing the way for telling Gloucester that a fiend (capable of speaking in different tones) led him to the top of a cliff and that his life has been saved by a miracle.
choughs, jackdaws.

gross, big.

Hangs, *i.e.* from a rope.

samphire, sea-fennel, then used as a pickle. The gathering of samphire on the cliffs of Dover was a regular trade in Shakespeare's day. The circumstantial detail supplied by Edgar would help to make the imaginary scene more real to Gloucester.

to her cock, to the size of her cockboat, or dinghy.

unnumber'd, innumerable. *Cf.* "unprized", "dishonour'd" and "untented", notes respectively pp. 53 and 60.

idle. See note p. 83.

the deficient sight Topple, on account of the deficient sight I topple.

another purse. See Gloucester's last speech but one in IV. i.

opposeless, unable to be opposed, irresistible.

snuff, remnant, *lit.* the charred, used up part of the wick (which would be "snuffed" with "snuffers"). Nothing to do with the word on p. 71.

conceit . . . theft, imagination ("conceit") may take a man's life away when he wants to die.

Thus. As Edgar mentioned above (aside).

pass, pass away.

What are you, sir? Here (and three and two lines above) Edgar pretends to be someone else—at the bottom of the cliff.

gossamer, a long single thread of a spider's web.

at each, *i.e.* end to end.

bourn, limit, boundary (to the sea). Not the same meaning as in note p. 77 (note on "Come . . . me").

a-height, on high. *Cf.* aloft.

gorged, throated.

wretchedness. *Cf.* "misery", note p. 66.

whelk'd, with swellings on them.

father. Notice the irony of this, which would (and does) appeal to the audience. Edgar calls Gloucester "father" three times more before the end of the scene.

clearest, purest.

men's impossibilities, things impossible to men.

free, *i.e.* free from affliction or anxiety.

safer, sounder, saner.

accommodate, cover. *Cf.* note on "unaccommodated", p. 75.

press-money, money for a conscripted soldier, "pressed" into service.

crow-keeper, scare-crow, or perhaps someone employed to keep off crows.

a clothier's yard, *i.e.* on your bow. *Cf. Chevy Chace,*

> "An arrow of a cloth-yard long
> Up to the head drew he."

bills, pikes.

clout, bull's eye. *Cf.* "blank", note p. 52.

word, *i.e.* password. See note p. 75.

white hairs . . . there, *i.e.* I was experienced while still a boy.

trick, distinguishing characteristic.

thy cause, the charge against you.

civet. See note on "cat", p. 75.

piece, masterpiece.

squiny, squint.

blind Cupid. Cupid, the god of love, was represented as blind in classical mythology, and still it is reputed that "love is blind". It is a pathetic touch that Lear takes Gloucester to be a woman "making eyes" at him.

case, *i.e.* socket.

are you there with me? Do you follow me?

heavy. Punning on "serious", "bad".

handy-dandy, take your pick. The name of a game in which children tried to guess in which hand a certain article was held.

creature, *i.e.* beggar.

cozener, cheat, *lit.* one who pretends to be man's "cousin" (relative) in order to get something out of him, a form of confidence trick as common in Elizabethan times as to-day. The implication in this line is that when the usurer has the authority of the law on his side he hangs the "cozener", but really he is just as bad as the cozener.

able 'em, make them able (to get out of the law).

that. Imagined to be money.

the power . . . lips. By giving money.

politician, schemer.

impertinency, irrelevancy.

This', this is.

block. Lear has taken his hat off, and this leads him to think of the block on which it was fashioned, and so to the felt of which it was made.

stol'n, come quietly.

kill. This was the word of command for a charge in Shakespeare's day.

natural fool. As we say, "a born fool".

salt, *i.e.* tears.

bravely, in fine fashion. See note on "brave", p. 72.

smug, spruce, well-groomed. (There was nothing censorious in the meaning in Shakespeare's day.)

there's life in't. *Cf.* our phrase, "There's life in it yet!"

speed you, *i.e.* God speed you.

vulgar, common knowledge.

main descry, espial of the main body.

Stands on the hourly thought, is certainly hourly expected. *Cf.* "Stand in hard cure", note p. 77.

Though that. See note on "Since that", p. 53.

on special cause, *i.e.* to look after Lear.

take my breath from me, *i.e.* by a natural death.

art, experience.

feeling sorrows, *i.e.* sorrows which are felt.

pregnant to, ready for. See note p. 63.

biding, dwelling-place.

To boot, into the bargain, in addition to (his thanks).

To raise my fortunes. Regan had promised preferment to the man who should murder Gloucester (IV. v. 38).

thyself remember, *i.e.* remember (and confess) your sins.

friendly. Because death is just what Gloucester desires.

the infection . . . thee, you catch his bad fortune.
gait, way.
chud, I would.
zwaggered, blustered (swaggered).
che vor ye, I warn you.
ise, I shall.
costard, head (slang), *lit.* a kind of apple. *Cf.* "nut" today.
ballow, cudgel.
chill, I will.
foins, thrusts (in fencing).
Leave, *i.e.* by your leave.
want not, be not lacking. See note p. 84.
fruitfully, *i.e.* plentifully, abundantly. The next sentence shows that Goneril was thinking that the coming battle would give Edmund plenty of opportunities.
undistinguish'd space, indistinguishable reach, *i.e.* no one knows how far it can go.
rake up, *i.e.* bury. Oswald had asked him to bury his body.
post. See note p. 67.
lechers, adulterers.
death-practised duke, duke whose death has been plotted. *Cf.* "practices" (the noun), note p. 56.
ingenious, conscious.
distract. The past participle.
griefs, injuries, hardships, grievances.
bestow. See note p. 70.

ACT IV. SCENE VII

Cordelia is present as Lear, under the doctor's care, half comes to his senses. The scene opens with her sincere thanks to Kent.

Her concern for her father's welfare stands out against the savage treatment inflicted on him by Goneril and Regan, as the soft music contrasts with the fury of the elements when Lear was on the heath. This is the quietest—and happiest—scene in the play.

soft music. Always believed to be soothing in afflictions of the mind.
modest. See note p. 67.
weeds, clothes.
memories, memorials.
Yet, already, so soon.
made intent, resolved intention.
wind up. Metaphor from tightening the strings of a musical instrument.
child-changed, changed by his children.
temperance, calmness.
Thy medicine, *i.e.* medicine to cure thee.
not. The emphasis in on this word.

these white flakes, *i.e.* Lear's white hair.
cross, *i.e.* forked.
perdu, lost one (Fr.).
this thin helm, *i.e.* Lear's "white flakes".
Mine enemy's dog . . . fire. *Cf.* Gloucester's words in the speech before he had his eyes put out (III. vii).
short, inadequate, in short supply.
all. See note p. 52.
that, so that.
wide, *i.e.* wide of the mark.
abused. See note p. 80.
And, to . . . mind. These two short irregular lines correspond to the unsettled state of Lear's mind.
mainly, quite.
skill, sense. See ll. 21-22.
even o'er, connect together.
They say . . . Germany. A very natural touch that adds reality. Further, Kent had said (I. i) that he would "shape his old course in a country new".
arbitrement, decision.
point and period, aim and end.
Or . . . or, either . . . or.

REVISION QUESTIONS ON ACT IV

1. Illustrate how one of the effects of Gloucester's suffering is to make him think of others in distress, even as Lear did.

2. Contrast the attitude of Goneril and of Albany to the danger of foreign invasion.

3. "One way I like this well." What way?

4. What is the *dramatic* reason for the return of the King of France to his own country?

5. What is shown (*a*) of Regan's character, (*b*) of Oswald's, when they meet in this Act?

6. How does Edgar make the "cliff" seem real to Gloucester?

7. "Lear misunderstood all his daughters, but none so much as Cordelia." Illustrate this statement from the two scenes in which she appears in this Act.

ACT V. SCENE I

Goneril and Regan show more concern over their chances of winning Edmund than over the result of the coming battle.

Albany must dispel an invader, but has no zest (because he has no conscience) for the fight.

Edgar (still in disguise) hands Albany a letter (Goneril's letter to Edmund, that he took from Oswald).

Before he goes off to the battle Edmund considers his position.

> To both these sisters have I sworn my love,
> Each jealous of the other, as the stung
> Are of the adder. Which of them shall I take?

He seems to think that his best plan is to use Albany's "countenance for the battle", and then "let her who would be rid of him devise his speedy taking off".

since, since then.

man, servant (Oswald).

miscarried. A euphemism for "dead".

doubted, feared. *Cf.* "doubtful", l. 10.

conjunct. See note p. 65.

bosom'd with her, in her confidence. *Cf.* "of her bosom", note p. 84.

as far as we call hers, to such an extent that we may call you hers.

dear my lord. See note on "Good my lord", p. 51.

Fear. See note p. 71. Not the meaning of the word in the notes on pp. 76 and 81.

for, as for.

as, in so far as.

bolds, emboldens (by lending him support), *i.e.* not in so far as France supports the king.

ancient, long-experienced.

you'll go with us? And not with Edmund! "Us" is the regal plural (*cf.* "our", IV. ii. 1).

convenient, proper.

the riddle, *i.e.* what you are after, what you have in mind.

machination ceases, *i.e.* plotting against your life must necessarily cease with your death.

o'erlook. See note on "o'er-read. o'er-looking", p. 55, and *cf.* "o'erskip", note p. 78. There is no consistency in the use of the hyphen.

We will greet the time. This is a mild rebuke, as much as to say, "I will greet the time *when it comes*", I will take things as they come.

jealous, suspicious.

carry out my side, play my hand successfully (a metaphor from cards).

countenance, authority.

taking off. Like "miscarried" (l. 5) a euphemism for "death"—here "murder". Even Edmund cannot look the deed in the face and recognise it for what it would be—sheer murder.

my state, the position in which I am.

Stands on, requires. *Cf.* note on "Stand in hard cure", p. 77.

Act V. Scene ii

The battle is soon over, and Edgar tells Gloucester that "King Lear hath lost, he and his daughter ta'en".

Ripeness, *i.e.* readiness.

Act V. Scene iii

Lear and Cordelia pass over the stage as Edmund's prisoners.   There is no doubt of Lear's devotion to Cordelia now.   After they have gone away under guard, Edmund gives secret orders for their murder.

Albany appears with Goneril and Regan, and after some bickering between the two sisters concerning their right to Edmund, Albany proclaims Edmund a traitor, and if no one else appears he vows that he will prove it on his heart. But someone else does appear—Edgar, who succeeds in vanquishing his half-brother, who is mortally wounded in the duel.

Meanwhile Regan has been taken ill—poisoned by Goneril.   Then Albany produces Goneril's letter, and, after snatching at it to try and tear it up, Goneril goes out and commits suicide.

In death Edmund repents—"Some good I mean to do, despite of mine own nature", and makes it known that his "writ is on the life of Lear and on Cordelia".   The news comes in time to save Lear, but not Cordelia.   Lear carries in her body, but his grief in her death is too much for him, and he too dies (see p. 21).

Albany offers the kingdom to Kent and Edgar, but Kent indicates that, like Lear's, his life's work is over. So at the end it is left to Albany and Edgar to arrange things for the good of "the gored state".

Like most Shakespearean tragedies the play ends on a note of hope.   The past seems like a nightmare, but there are signs that the future of Britain is in safer hands.   The world must go on and there are men to show it the way, men not so overpowering perhaps, but more capable in handling day to day affairs.

their greater pleasures . . . That, the pleasures of those greater persons who.
censure. See note p. 76.

these daughters and these sisters. Notice that Cordelia nowhere calls her sisters by name. This is a little touch that is scarcely noticed, yet has its effect in emphasising the estrangement between her and them. Similarly Lear here refers to his two daughters as "them" (l. 25).

in, *i.e.* in favour.

the mystery, *i.e.* the explanation of the mystery.

God. The gods are mentioned many times in *King Lear*, God only here. This is one of the things that helps to give to the play its barbarous atmosphere.

packs, confederacies. *Cf.* "packings", note p. 71.

ebb ... moon, *i.e.* are quickly out and in (like the tides).

fire us hence like foxes, *i.e.* as foxes are driven from their holes by fire (or smoke).

The good-years. A word used for an indefinite evil power, corresponding to "the plague" or "the devil".

fell, hide, skin.

starve, die (by any means, not necessarily lack of food).

write happy, *i.e.* you will have made yourself happy, set the seal of happiness upon it (made "thy way to noble fortunes").

man's work, *i.e.* and not the work of an animal (who would "draw a cart" and "eat dried oats"). Edmund intends to forestall "the mercy which he [Albany] intends to Lear and to Cordelia", as he said he would at the end of Sc. i. If Lear lived, Edmund's ambition to be chief of state, married to Goneril, might be imperilled.

the common bosom, the feelings of the common people. *Cf.* note on "bosom'd with her", p. 90.

impress'd, conscripted. See note on "press-money", p. 86.

lances. Metonymy ("lances" for the men who bear them).

the queen, *i.e.* of France.

session. *Cf.* the use of the word in law to-day, *e.g.* Quarter Sessions.

Not as a brother. So far Edmund has spoken to Albany as if he were his equal—"I thought it fit", "*our* impress'd lances".

immediacy, position of immediate authority (for Regan), not a delegated authority.

grace, gracious qualities. A sneering pun on Regan's use of the word.

compeers, equals.

the most. Referring to Regan's "the best".

That eye ... a-squint. Alluding to an old proverb, "Love being jealous makes a good eye look a-squint". A heartless comment to one to whom she has already given poison, such as we should expect from Goneril.

stomach. Supposed to be the seat of anger (as the liver was of courage—see note on "lily-livered", p. 64).

General. She addresses Edmund.

the walls are thine. A metaphor from the complete surrender of a town.

let-alone, prevention.

in thine attaint, together with your impeachment.

bans, *i.e.* marriage-bans. Not the meaning in note p. 67, which derives from the same word (meaning "proclamations") used in the Pope's proclamations of excommunication.

interlude, touch of comedy, *lit.* a short play—usually of a comic nature—performed between other affairs, *e.g.* at a banquet (Lat. "inter" = between, "ludere" = to play). Hence used generally of any comic touch intervening in more serious matters.

Throwing down a glove. The way of making a formal challenge. If the person challenged picked up the glove it was a sign that he accepted the challenge.

virtue, power, valour. *Cf.* note p. 84.

degree, rank.

cope, encounter, cope with.

mine honours, *i.e.* my knighthood.

Maugre, in spite of, "despite" (Fr. "malgré").

fire-new, brand-new (a corresponding metaphor).

heart, *i.e.* spirit.

Conspirant, conspiring. A French form retaining the ending of the French present participle.

descent, *i.e.* lowest descent, in antithesis to "extremest upward".

most toad-spotted traitor, *i.e.* as treacherous as the toad is spotted. A slimy creature like the toad (and one thought to be venomous) suits the context.

whereto, against which.

that. Linked with "since"—since that. See note on "Since that", p. 53.

say, assay, proof.

nicely, *i.e.* by the precise "rule of knighthood". See note p. 65.

hell-hated, hated like hell.

Save him. Albany stops the fight so as to prove Edmund's guilt by Goneril's letter.

cozen'd. See note on "cozener", p. 37.

Hold. An exclamation, corresponding to "There!" or "Now!"

the laws are mine, not thine, *i.e.* I make the laws, not you. It is I who am chief in the state.

Ask . . . know. The Folios give this speech to Edmund, and the Quartos (see p. 48) to Goneril. It makes good sense in the mouth of either. It is perhaps more likely that Albany's question was addressed to Edmund, since he has held up the letter for Goneril to see and her actions have shown that she was the writer—"I perceive you know it", he says. On the other hand, Edmund could not possibly have seen it before, so why should Albany ask him whether he knows it?

exchange charity, *i.e.* forgive each other. See note on "charity", p. 73.

The wheel. See note on "turn thy wheel!", p. 66.

I am here, *i.e.* as a result of "the wheel's" coming "full circle".

habit, dress. *Cf.* Fr. "habit".

success, issue, result.

flaw'd, broken. *Cf.* note on "flaws", p. 70.

passion, emotion, strong feeling (of any kind). *Cf.* Christ's "passion" in Gethsemane.

period. See note p. 89.

another, *i.e.* another sorrow.

puissant, powerful, strong.

Produce, bring in (*lit.* forward).

my writ . . . Cordelia. See ll. 27-40.

fordid, destroyed.

stone, *i.e.* crystal mirror.

end, *i.e.* of the world.

Fall, and cease! *I.e.* let the heavens fall and the world end now!

loved and hated, *i.e.* successively.

One of them, *i.e.* Lear. (The other was himself.)

your first of difference, the beginning of your change (in fortune).

Nor no man else, *i.e.* here is no welcome for me or anyone else. Notice the alliteration of *d* in this passage, giving a dull, deadly effect.

Your eldest . . . themselves. See note on "bending", p. 82.

bootless, useless. *Cf.* "To boot", note p. 87. The word is used again in l. 302.

O, see. There is a change in the King's appearance.

fool, innocent. Cordelia, undoubtedly, is meant. She is the only one in his thoughts.

undo this button. Lear imagines that the stuffiness he feels comes from his clothes too tight about him. It is in a touch like this that Shakespeare shows himself so great a dramatist. A lesser playwright might have forgotten Lear's humanity in his kingship. Lear feels difficulty in breathing, as any old man might have done, and such a natural touch relates the tragedy to the life which is the life of all of us, and therefore makes Lear seem more real, part and parcel of the common humanity we know, not a remote king in a world of his own.

pass. See note p. 86.

My master, *i.e.* Lear.

The weight . . . long. The final speech is given to Edgar in the Folios and to Albany in the Quartos. It is more fittingly Edgar's. Albany has spoken to Kent and Edgar. Kent, as the older man, replies first, and then it is only natural that Edgar should follow.

REVISION QUESTIONS ON ACT V

1. Give illustrations of Edmund's deceit in this Act.

2. Contrast the battle scene with any other of which you know in Shakespeare. Do you find the one in this play convincing?

3. In what way does Albany appear a different man from the Albany of Act I?

4. "An interlude!" What occasioned this exclamation by Goneril (Sc. iii)?

5. Comment on the extreme pathos of the last part of the play, between Lear's entrance with Cordelia dead in his arms and his own death. How is this pathos achieved—or emphasised—dramatically?

QUESTIONS

1. What is gained by bringing the Gloucester story into *King Lear*? Show how Shakespeare interweaves the two stories, setting down all the points of contact between the two.

2. Describe the part played by letters in *King Lear*.

3. "The theme of the play is the relationship of parents and children, with particular emphasis on the ungrateful child" (p. 13). Show how Shakespeare handles this theme.

4. Discuss the importance of the storm scenes in *King Lear*.

5.
> *Regan.* 'Tis the infirmity of his age: yet he hath ever but slenderly known himself.
> *Goneril.* The best and soundest of his time hath been but rash.

Is this dialogue an adequate clue to Lear's character?

6. Do you agree that Lear was "more sinn'd against than sinning"?

7. Comment on the suggestion that the play of *King Lear* might well be called "The Redemption of Lear".

8. How far is King Lear a characteristic Shakespearean tragic hero?

9. To what extent do you consider Cordelia responsible for the tragedy of *King Lear*?

10. Compare and contrast the character of Cordelia with that of *either* Goneril *or* Regan.

11. Contrast Goneril with Regan, and Albany with Cornwall.

12. Sketch the development of Gloucester's character in the play, comparing it with the development of the character of Lear.

13.

> As flies to wanton boys, are we to the gods;
> They kill us for their sport.

> The gods are just, and of our pleasant vices
> Make instruments to plague us.

Which of these quotations represents your reading of *King Lear*?

14. Edmund says of his own ending, "The wheel is come full circle". How far is this also true of the fate of Lear, Gloucester and Cordelia?

15.

> This is some fellow,
> Who . . . . doth affect
> A saucy roughness, and constrains the garb
> Quite from his nature: he cannot flatter, he,
> An honest mind and plain, he must speak truth!

How far do you consider this a correct and sufficient estimate of the character of Kent?

16. "This is not altogether fool, my lord." Discuss the dramatic function of the fool in the light of this remark.

17. Point out the significance of each of the following quotations.

> (*a*) To your professed bosoms I commit him:
> But yet, alas, stood I within his grace,
> I would prefer him to a better place.
> So, farewell to you both.

> (*b*) Since my young lady's going into France, sir, the fool
> hath much pined away.

> (*c*)   Ay, though thou didst produce
> My very character,—I'd turn it all
> To thy suggestion, plot, and damned practice.

> (*d*) One side will mock another; the other too.

18. In the popular eighteenth-century version *King Lear* was given a happy ending, in which Lear was restored to his kingdom and Edgar was married to Cordelia. Say what you think of Shakespeare's ending contrasted with this one.

19. "The language of poetry is metaphor." Do you agree with this? Give your reasons, with illustrations from *King Lear*.

20. Mention any features of *King Lear* that were conditioned by the theatre for which Shakespeare wrote.

CONTEXT QUESTIONS

Answer the questions upon the following passages.

1.   Such smiling rogues as these,
Like rats, oft bite the holy cords a-twain
Which are too intrinse t'unloose; smooth every
    passion
That in the natures of their lords rebel;
Bring oil to fire, snow to their colder moods;
Renege, affirm, and turn their halcyon beaks
With every gale and vary of their masters,
Knowing nought, like dogs, but following.
A plague upon your epileptic visage!

> (a) Give the meaning of the passage as closely as you can
> in your own words.
>
> (b) "Oft bite the holy cords a-twain which are too intrinse
> t'unloose." Is there any justification for the suspicion
> that this "smiling rogue" has encouraged the break
> between Lear and his daughters?
>
> (c) Explain, "Turn their halcyon beaks with every gale and
> vary of their masters".
>
> (d) "Knowing nought, like dogs, but following." Would
> you say that this was a just description of this par-
> ticular rogue? Give at least one example from the
> play in your answer.
>
> (e) "A plague upon your epileptic visage!" What occa-
> sioned this outburst?

2.   [*Kneeling*] O you mighty gods!
This world I do renounce, and, in your sights,
Shake patiently my great affliction off:
If I could bear it longer, and not fall
To quarrel with your great opposeless wills,
My snuff and loathed part of nature should
Burn itself out. If Edgar live, O, bless him!
Now, fellow, fare thee well.   [*He falls forward*

> (a) "You mighty gods!" The gods are often mentioned in
> *King Lear*, God only once. What is the effect of
> this?
>
> (b) "Patiently." Do you agree that Gloucester was
> patient? What, after this incident (irrespective of
> your answer to the first part of this question), made
> him *more* patient to endure?

(c) Explain "opposeless", "snuff".

(d) Where was Edgar at this time?

(e) This scene can easily become ridiculous. What helps, or can help, to make it serious—as Shakespeare intended it should be?

(f) Mention a *successful* attempt at suicide in the play, and say in what different spirit from this one that attempt appears to have been made.

3. Thou think'st 'tis much that this contentious storm
Invades us to the skin: so 'tis to thee;
But where the greater malady is fix'd,
The lesser is scarce felt.   Thou'dst shun a bear;
But if thy flight lay toward the roaring sea,
Thou'dst meet the bear i' the mouth.   When the mind's free
The body's delicate; the tempest in my mind
Doth from my senses take all feeling else
Save what beats there.   Filial ingratitude!
Is it not as this mouth should tear this hand
For lifting food to't?   But I will punish home:
No, I will weep no more.   In such a night
To shut me out!   Pour on; I will endure.

(a) Give the meaning of the passage as closely as you can in your own words.

(b) "The tempest in my mind." What is the dramatic relation of the tempest in Lear's mind and the tempest on the heath?

(c) Point out a phrase in this passage which might be taken as the theme of *King Lear*, with a few brief comments on its fitness.

(d) "I will punish home." "I will endure." Give another instance where Lear decides to allow submission to take the place of revenge.

4.   *Edmund.*   Yet Edmund was beloved:
The one the other poison'd for my sake,
And after slew herself.
     Albany.   Even so.   Cover their faces.
     Edmund.   I pant for life: some good I mean to do,
Despite of mine own nature.   Quickly send,
Be brief in it, to the castle; for my writ
Is on the life of Lear and on Cordelia:
Nay, send in time.

(a) "Yet Edmund was beloved." There is a wealth of meaning in these four words. Why should Edmund in particular value affection?

(b) The decision made in Edmund's second speech follows naturally from his thoughts in the first. How?

(c) When reminded of it, what did Edmund send as a token that the cancellation of his order was genuine?

(d) How had Edmund proposed to account for the death of Cordelia?

5. No, Regan, thou shalt never have my curse:
Thy tender-hefted nature shall not give
Thee o'er to harshness: her eyes are fierce, but thine
Do comfort and not burn. 'Tis not in thee
To grudge my pleasures, to cut off my train,
To bandy hasty words, to scant my sizes,
And in conclusion to oppose the bolt
Against my coming in: thou better know'st
The offices of nature, bond of childhood,
Effects of courtesy, dues of gratitude;
Thy half o' the kingdom hast thou not forgot,
Wherein I thee endow'd.

(a) Why does the passage begin with "No"? With what is Lear disagreeing?

(b) Show in detail how every one of Lear's prophecies was falsified, and that before very long.

(c) What is the most unworthy reason of those given by Lear for expecting his daughter's consideration? Why?

(d) What in the description of Regan is consistent with her being a *weaker* character than Goneril?

(e) Explain "tender-hefted", "sizes", "offices", "effects".

6. Fairest Cordelia, that art most rich, being poor;
Most choice, forsaken; and most loved, despised!
Thee and thy virtues here I seize upon:
Be it lawful I take up what's cast away.
Gods, gods! 'tis strange that from their cold'st neglect
My love should kindle to inflamed respect.
Thy dowerless daughter, king, thrown to my chance,
Is queen of us, of ours, and our fair France:
Not all the dukes of waterish Burgundy
Can buy this unprized precious maid of me.

Bid them farewell, Cordelia, though unkind:
Thou losest here, a better where to find.

    (*a*) What decision had Cordelia come to immediately before this speech?

    (*b*) What does Lear say immediately after it?

    (*c*) Explain "waterish".

    (*d*) In what sense was Cordelia "unprized", and to what does this refer?

    (*e*) Why is the second part of this speech in heroic couplets?

    (*f*) Comment on the style of the passage, irrespective of the rhyme.

7. Had you not been their father, these white flakes
Had challeng'd pity of them. Was this a face
To be expos'd against the warring winds?
To stand against the deep dread-bolted thunder?
In the most terrible and nimble stroke
Of quick cross lightning? to watch—poor perdu!—
With this thin helm? *Mine enemy's dog,*
Though he had bit me, should have stood that night
Against my fire. And wast thou fain, poor father,
To hovel thee with swine and rogues forlorn,
In short and musty straw?

    (*a*) Give the meaning of this passage as closely as you can in your own words.

    (*b*) "Of them." Of whom?

    (*c*) Explain "perdu".

    (*d*) What does the passage show of Cordelia s character?

    (*e*) Who else in the play uses an almost identical illustration to that in italics?

    (*f*) Give examples of alliteration in this passage, and say what is their effect when spoken.

8.   We'll set thee to school to an ant, to teach thee there's no labouring i' the winter. All that follow their noses are led by their eyes but blind men; and there's not a nose among twenty but can smell him that's stinking. Let go thy hold when a great wheel runs down a hill, lest it break thy neck with following it; but the great one that goes up the hill, let him draw thee after. When a wise man gives thee better counsel, give me mine again: I would have none but knaves follow it, since a fool gives it.

    (a) To what question (or questions) was this an answer?

    (b) Apply the Fool's illustrations to the fortunes of Lear
        (or those of his followers).

    (c) Does the Fool follow his own counsel?

    (d) Why is this passage in prose?

    (e) Comment on the prose style.

9. And my poor fool is hang'd!   No, no, no life!
Why should a dog, a horse, a rat, have life,
And thou no breath at all?   Thou'lt come no more,
Never, never, never, never, never!
Pray you, undo this button: thank you, sir.
Do you see this?   Look on her, look, her lips,
Look there, look there!

    (a) Whom do you think Lear means by his "fool"?

    (b) What is the effect of the repetition in l. 4?

    (c) What is the dramatic effect of Lear's thinking about
        such an ordinary thing as a button at a moment
        like this?

    (d) "Look there, look there!"   In what tone of voice do
        you imagine that Lear says these two words?

    (e) This has been called the most pathetic episode in the
        play.   Would you agree?

10.   *Oswald.*   Slave, thou hast slain me: villain, take
      my purse:
If ever thou wilt thrive, bury my body;
And give the letters which thou find'st about me
To Edmund Earl of Gloucester; seek him out
Upon the British party.   O, untimely death! [*Dies.*
    Edgar.   I know thee well: a serviceable villain;
As duteous to the vices of thy mistress
As badness would desire.

    (a) Does Edgar bury Oswald's body?

    (b) "The letters."   One of them has an important bearing
        on the plot.   How?

    (c) "A serviceable villain."   Is this a true estimate of
        Oswald's character?   Give at least one example to
        illustrate your answer.

    (d) Is the word "villain" used with the same meaning by
        both speakers?

(e) "O, untimely death!" Why would Oswald regard his death as particularly untimely at this moment? What does this show of his character?

(f) What does Edgar do with the letter that he finds on Oswald?

(g) Mention any other incident in the play depending on or concerned with a letter.

11.   Go to; say you nothing. There's a division betwixt the dukes; and a worse matter than that: I have received a letter this night; 'tis dangerous to be spoken; I have locked the letter in my closet: these injuries the king now bears will be revenged *home*; there's part of a *power* already footed: we must incline to the king. I will seek him, and privily relieve him: go you and maintain talk with the duke, that my *charity* be not of him perceived: if he ask for me, I am ill, and gone to bed. Though I die for it, as no less is threatened me, the king my old master must be relieved. There is some strange thing *toward*, Edmund; pray you, be careful.

(a) Explain the meaning of the words in italics.

(b) Show, *from this passage only*, how Gloucester's motives are a curious mixture of compassion and worldly wisdom.

(c) Do you consider it wrong of Gloucester to have relieved the King "privily", or should he have declared himself openly? Apart from the rights and wrongs of the matter, do you consider it the more sensible way of helping the King?

(d) Who else in the play has already mentioned (i) the "division betwixt the dukes", (ii) the "power" from abroad, and on what occasion?

(e) Point out an example of dramatic irony in this passage.

12. Wisdom and goodness to the vile seem vile:
Filths savour but themselves. What have you done?
Tigers, not daughters, what have you perform'd?
A father, and a gracious aged man,
Whose reverence even the head-lugg'd bear would lick,
Most barbarous, most degenerate! have you madded.
Could my good brother suffer you to do it?
A man, a prince, by him so benefited!
If that the heavens do not their visible spirits

Send quickly down to tame these vile offences,
It will come,
Humanity must perforce prey on itself,
Like monsters of the deep.

(a) Give the meaning of the passage as closely as you can
in your own words.

(b) What is the reply and the attitude of Goneril to this
reproach?

(c) The speaker was ignorant of the fate of his "good
brother". When did he find out about it?

(d) Comment briefly on the animal imagery of *King Lear*.

(e) What is the purpose of the short line (l. 11)?

KEY TO CONTEXT QUESTIONS

(1) II. ii. *Kent*, (2) IV. vi. 34-41, (3) III. iv. 6-18, (4) V. iii,
241-249, (5) II. iv. *Lear*, (6) I. i. *France*, (7) IV. vii. 30-40,
(8) II. iv. *Fool*, (9) V. iii. 307-313, (10) IV. vi, (11) III. iii.
Gloucester, (12) IV. ii. 38-50.